Freemasonry in All Ages

Also from Westphalia Press

westphaliapress.org

Freemasonry in All Ages

by M.F. Carey

Edited and introduced by
Guillermo De Los Reyes

WESTPHALIA PRESS
An imprint of Policy Studies Organization

Freemasonry in All Ages

Westphalia Press
An imprint of Policy Studies Organization
1527 New Hampshire Ave., NW
Washington, D.C. 20036
dgutierrezs@ipsonet.org

ISBN-13: 978-1935907435
ISBN-10: 1935907433

Cover design by Taillefer Long at Illuminated Stories:
www.illuminatedstories.com

Updated material and comments on this edition
can be found at the Westphalia Press website:
www.westphaliapress.org

Introduction to the New Edition

JUST HOW OLD IS FREEMASONRY?

Reverend M.F. Carey was an Episcopalian priest and enthusiastic Freemason who served parishes in Nebraska, including the still existent St. Thomas Episcopal Church in Falls City. He was born in Tralee, County Kerry, Ireland in 1841 and in 1869 entered Trinity College in Dublin, the elite Protestant university. He was ordained by the Bishop of Kilmore and emigrated to America in 1881.

At the time he wrote *Freemasonry in All Ages*, Masonic scholarship was in a time of great flux and the book displays the changes taking place. The romantic school of Masonic historiography, which gave highly fanciful accounts of the origins of the fraternity was being challenged by a more scientific and scholarly approach. Carey is careful to straddle the two approaches, anxious to relate a good many of the rather folkloric theories of origin while conceding more realistic possibilities. And as a clergyman, he attempts to maintain a Christian view of Freemasonry while acknowledging its deistic and Enlightenment affinities.

E

This then is very much a work of its time, reflecting the difficulties of bringing to bear modern research techniques on a subject that thrived on imaginative accounts. The tension between the two schools of thought continues to this day.

Guillermo De Los Reyes
University of Houston

F

Freemasonry in All Ages

BEING

A SKETCH

OF ITS

HISTORY, PHILOSOPHY, AND ETHICAL TEACHING,

BY

REV. M. F. CAREY,

ASSOCIATE OF THE PHILOSOPHICAL SOCIETY
OF GREAT BRITAIN.

———————

AUTHOR OF BIBLOS, THE OLDEST BOOK IN THE WORLD, ETC

———————

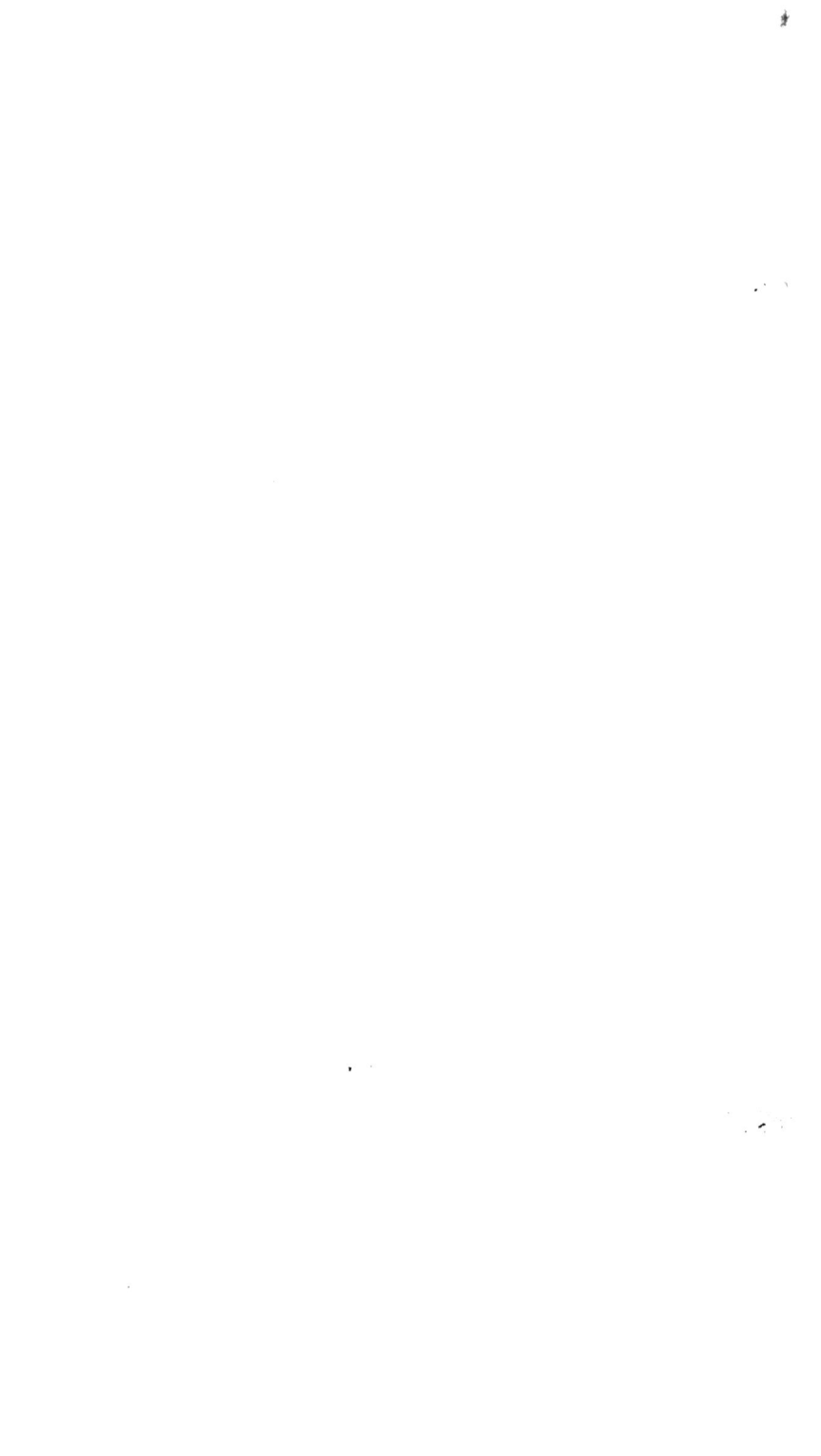

TABLE OF CONTENTS.

"Let there be light!   O God I need it.
Let there be light!   O Father speed it.
And grant that wisdom, from above,
My heart may fill with perfect love.
Lead me heavenly Father, lead me,
And let me feel that peace doth rest
Upon my soul.   Then I am blessed:
And o'er my pathway let there shine
The heavenly rays of light Divine,
To help me e'er to do thy will:
And let me hear thy 'peace be still'!
Show me the work that Thou hast given
Thy servant here to do for heaven:
And help me heavenly Father feel
For other's woes, and other's ills,
That I be fully fitted here
To live with Thee in yon bright sphere.
Help so to live that I can say,
'Thy will be done,' without a fear;
Lamb of God I pray Thee hear
And answer this, an earnest prayer."

FREEMASONRY IN ALL AGES.

CHAPTER I.

Every Mason knows that in each Lodge of Free and Accepted Masons, there is placed in a conspicuous position, so that every eye may behold it, a Divine luminary, known and designated as a " Great Light."

This "Great Light" is set as a beacon illuminating the whole mind and spirit of man. It is a repository of the most sublime truths and the most ennobling thoughts that can possibly be presented to his mind. No where else in the world can such precious, distilled wisdom, be found.

The mightiest intellects the world has produced, have paid lowly reverence to the far-reaching depth of this wisdom. The *humble spirit* only can see and truly appreciate the glorious truths and light it contains. To such it is ever "a lamp to their feet and a light to their path," illuminating them

through the dark wastes and rugged paths
of this life's journey.

This light reveals to us a wondrous volume
of truth. From its place in the " centre of
the Lodge, it pours forth upon the East, the
South, and the West, its refulgent rays of
Divine truth." It is used among Masons as
the symbol of the will of God.

It is a Revelation from God to Man.

The great facts it reveals have been, with
greater or less purity, preserved and incorporated in all the great religious systems of
the world.

The first great fact it reveals is that *God
is the great Architect of the Universe.* The
sublime language used to express this is:
" In the beginning God created the heaven
and the earth."

The sacred historian recounts the suc-
cessive periods or " days " which were
employed by the Great Architect in bringing the earth to its present state, and fitting
it to become the abode of man. The fiat of
the Almighty on the first day was: " Let

there be light, and there was light." He
ends with the remarkable and emphatic
statement: " Let us make man, in our own
image, after our likeness."

So man was made in the image of God.
As a corollary to this great fact, we are
justified in assuming that man was created
in a state of innocence. The fact, however,
is revealed to us that man, through the sin
of disobedience, lost his primeval innocency.
And that by sin he became estranged in his
mind from God, his Creator. But now is
unfolded to him the wondrous scheme of
Redemption and Reconciliation. Now is
the promise of the Redeemer and Saviour
given, that the " Seed of the woman should
bruise the serpent's head." This Redeemer
was to be the God-man — the Son of God,
and the Son of Man — that is, *of our
Humanity.*

He was "the Word which was made
flesh." " He tabernacled among us." He
was the " true light which lighteth every
man that cometh into the world." He truly
" brought life and immortality to light."

By Him was effected the Restoration of Man.

By His life and death He made atonement for sin. By His glorious Resurrection He triumphed over death and the grave. "He led captivity captive." "He ascended into heaven, and sits at the right hand of God — from whence He shall come to judge the quick and the dead."

But the "Great Light" further reveals to us the glorious, all-comforting truth, that God is not only our Creator, but that He is our Father in Heaven, and that we are His children. It proclaims, too, the great fact of the Universality of the Fatherhood of God, and the Universality of the Brotherhood of Man. These grand truths are received and especially emphasized by the Fraternity of Freemasons, not as a mere rhetorical expression, but as a precious revelation of the relation of God to His children, and of the relation which His children should bear to one another.

Here we may state that the great leading facts of Revelation are, the Unity of God, Immortality, Redemption, Resurrec-

tion, Man's Responsibility and Accountability; and as a consequence — *a future
judgment.*

These prominent facts of Revelation have
been incorporated in all the great religious
systems that we have knowledge of. They
formed the basic principles of their philosophy.

We know that in every age of the world's
history, the ablest minds, the profoundest
thinkers, the wisest philosophers, have occupied themselves with the solution of the
problem of the existence of man on this
earth, and his future destiny. From their
investigation have arisen the various philosophical speculations and forms of religious
beliefs which have ever been received by
men.

As we proceed in our investigation of
these *ancient* philosophies, we will perceive
that, though the germs of the truth were
preserved, yet, as the world grew older, the
scope of their teaching was but as a dim
light in a thick mist in comparison to the
refulgent rays of the "Son of Righteousness," arising, illuminating the world with

Divine light and truth. "He spake as never man spoke." He was the truest light that ever shone in our darkness, and His message to men is the highest and purest, the profoundest and simplest, that has ever been spoken. He came from the bosom of the Father. He was the manifestation of God to man. The loftiest ideals of moral grandeur that had ever been spoken or promulgated by man are pitiable in comparison to the life of Christ. And His life reveals what the life of man may be when lived in unity with God, and what the life and character of God is in unity with man.

Thus, in Christ, all the Law and the Prophets, all the philosophies, all the "Mysteries" and religions, had their prototype and fulfillment.

We know that a spirit of inquiry and research in every department of human knowledge is characteristic of the present age. Physical science is unfolding to us the mysteries and the treasures of nature. Astronomy is revealing to us a more extended knowledge of the Universe of God, and exhibiting the mighty, the stupendous works of the "Great Architect." Pure and applied mathematics are expanding the mind of man, leading him to vast and astounding discoveries in the realms of nature. The storehouses of history, too, in which were deposited the records of antiquity, are yielding up their secrets. A deep interest is being manifested in archæological explorations in Babylonia, Syria, Egypt, Phœnicia, Greece, and Rome. These have resulted in bringing to light precious documents of the past, throwing a flood of light on the history, art, science, religion, and daily social life of the nations of antiquity.

The stone libraries and terra-cotta tablets, found in mounds and other depositories in these countries, furnish the archæologist, the chronologist, the philologist, and the historian, with treasures of deeply interesting and valuable information.

The thousands of tablets found in the British Museum, Paris, Berlin, St. Petersburg, Constantinople, and other places, furnish the student of history and philology with long lost chapters of human history. Although, as might be expected, a great deal of unimportant matter is contained in these records; yet, they are of special value to every Mason, not alone because of the possible amount of light they may throw on the history of the Fraternity; but more especially *in this one particular* that the higher we go up the stream of human history, the clearer and stronger is the evidence, that from the earliest dawn of his existence, man has been a believer in One, Eternal Creator. Examining the most ancient records of Egypt, India, Babylonia, Syria, and China, we are confronted with this fact, that pure Monotheism was the one conception of the One God, and that this was evidenced from the very beginning of the religion of these nations.

It is true, indeed, that the belief in One, Personal God, was corrupted and debased, and that degrading and superstitious rites were introduced into the mode of worshipping God; but, in the beginning, the fountain of life and light was pure and clear, even as its Great Author.

The history of man from the first dawn of his existence proves him to have been a

religious being.   Exalted intellects, though
not professedly religious, bear testimony to
this fact.   Professor Tyndall, for instance,
says, in a speech delivered in Belfast, Ireland: "There is also that deep-set feeling
which, since the earliest dawn of history,
and, probably, for ages prior to all history,
incorporated itself into the religions of the
world.   *   *   The immovable basis of the
sentiment in the nature of man."

He also says: "Physical science can not
satisfy all the cravings of man's nature."

And Professor Max Müller says: "Wherever we find man we also find worship and
religion."

A question here arises, whence came this
religious feeling or instinct in man?   Different theories have been propounded, all alike
unsatisfactory and unscientific, excepting the
one that ascribes it to God by direct Revelation.

God, in the beginning, created man in His
own image; that is, he created him a moral
being.   From his moral nature springs the
consciousness of responsibility.   His moral
faculty endows him with the capability of

knowing God. Hence, a correspondence between the *nature* of God and the *nature* of man; and, hence also, the possibility of a Revelation of God to man."

According to natural law, when substances are chemically united, they must possess certain properties or qualities which is scientifically known as "*chemical affinity*." Without this affinity they will not coalesce. Water and oil will not coalesce, because there is no "chemical affinity" between them. So, too, some substances possess magnetic properties which attract others. The correspondence between the moral nature of man and his Creator creates a *spiritual* affinity by which the mind and spirit of man are attracted by the Eternal Spirit.

Observation and experience teach us that everything in nature has a *correlative*. The echo implies a voice or sound of some sort. Music implies some instrument which produces it. In the whole range of creation, is *man* alone to be the victim of a delusion? Is man alone to be mocked? What is the outcome of his thoughts, his hopes, his fears, the deep and intense yearnings of his soul?

Is there nothing outside of the finite and limited on which the lofty and infinite aspirations of his spirit can find a responsive objective? What is there in this life to completely satisfy the cravings of his nature? The response of every human heart is, *there is nothing.*

Is there, then, nothing real or tangible to form the goal of his desires? Or are these desires nothing but simply the " stuff that dreams are made of? " Surely, the whole history of man throughout the ages of his existence stamps this solution of the cravings of his being *as a lie.* " Be not deceived, God is not mocked," is the solemn language of the Apostle. Neither is man deceived. The yearnings of his spirit must have an objective end; *that objective end is God.*

And this forms the *foundation principles* of Freemasonry. All its symbols, teaching, philosophy, and general cultus are in consonance with, and designed throughout its whole history, not alone to conserve the great leading truths of Revelation, but to impress them, in the most solemn manner, on the minds of every member of the Fraternity.

From beginning to end of its entire system, those sublime truths are prominently set forth and emphasized.

And that these are not taught as mere abstract facts, or merely as a system of cold philosophy, but that they are vitalized and energized with the spirit of active benevolence, virtue, charity, and truth, we shall hereafter show.

It is a grand thought (and it is inconceivable otherwise) that the great leading facts of Revelation were incorporated, and, to a considerable extent, preserved, in all the great religious systems of antiquity. It is true that, as they come down the stream of ages, as we have before observed, they become obscured by gross practices; and what was once pure and holy became perverted to what was foul, enslaving, and demoralizing. Yet even in their most corrupt form their great central truths had never become wholly extinguished. They were preserved in the midst of corruption like gems scintillating in a mass of rubbish.

As before stated, we have the strongest possible testimony that in the beginning of his career man received a Revelation from his Creator. The nature and facts of this Revelation we must undoubtedly suppose were communicated by Adam to his descendants. Very early in the history of the race, however, we have accounts of the perversion of the Divine truths among some of his posterity. During the whole of the antediluvian period the truth was preserved in the direct descendants of Seth. The Bible expressly states this fact.

Noah, of the direct line of Seth, was the recipient of these truths. He communicated them to his sons. Thus the truth was transmitted either by oral tradition or by documentary records, or, more probably, *by both*, through the line of the antediluvian patriarchs; and by Noah and his sons (the survivors of the Deluge) to the post-diluvian patriarchs, and by them, in like manner, to their offspring; and thus we see how the truth was transmitted from generation to generation, through all the cycles of human history, from the remotest antiquity to the present day.

CHAPTER II.

In the Book of Genesis we are informed that the primitive fathers of mankind, from the time of the Deluge, wandered without fixed abode for some centuries. They settled at length in the land of Shinar, where they established themselves in a permanent abode. In this settled mode of life they experienced neither the changes nor vicissitudes which tend to the formation of a change of speech. *They were of one language and of one speech.* In this permanent settlement in Shinar, they found material suitable for the building of edifices. This consisted of clay which they burnt for brick and bitumen which they used for mortar. With these, they built a city, and *a tower of great elevation.* This tower has always been known as the " Tower of Babel." Babel, according to the authority of some etymologists, means confusion; according to others, Bab-El means the gate of El. That is, the gate of God. This last meaning is founded on the supposition that primarily a temple to the worship of the true God had been raised there; but that Nimrod became the first open apostate after the flood, from the worship of Jehovah. It is supposed, too, that it was through his instigation that the tower was built.

Various reasons are assigned for the building of the tower. Aben Ezra says: "Those who built the tower were not so insensate as to imagine that they could by any such means reach to heaven; nor yet fear another deluge, since they had the promise of God to the contrary; but they wished for a city which should be a common residence and a rendezvous, serving in the midst of the wide, open plains of Babylonia to prevent the traveler from losing his way — in order that while they took measures for their own convenience and advantage, they might also make themselves a name with future ages."

Another author, confirming the opinion of the above, says: "They erected a building large enough and as high that it might be a mark and a rallying point in the vast plains where they had settled, in order to prevent

their being scattered abroad, and thus the
ties of kindred be rudely severed, individuals
be involved in peril, and their numbers be
prematurely thinned at a time when population was weak and insufficient."

The Jewish historian, Josephus, quoting
the Sibyl, says: "When all men were of
one language and one speech, some of them
built high towers as if they would thereby
ascend to heaven, but the gods sent storms
of wind and overthrew the tower, and gave
everyone his peculiar language, and for this
reason it is said the city was called Babylon."

Again, the church historian, Eusebius,
quoting Abydemus, says: "That the first
men relying on their strength, built a high
tower reaching toward heaven, where the
city of Babylon was afterwards built.) The
gods brought the building down on their
heads, from the ruins of which Babylon was
built."

Birs Nimrud, on the west of the river
Euphrates, and six miles to the southwest of
the town of Hillah, is claimed as the most
probable site of the Tower of Babel.   It is
said that the traveler who has seen this Birs

Nimrud feels at once that, of the ruined mounds in this region, there is not one which so nearly corresponds with his preconceived ideas of the Tower of Babel as this. Mr. Rich gives the following description of it: "It is of an oblong form, the entire circumference of which is 762 yards. At the eastern side it is cloven by a deep furrow, and is not more than 50 or 60 feet high. On the summit is a solid pile of brick 37 feet high by 28 in breadth, diminishing in thickness to the top, which is broken and irregular, and rent by a fissure extending through a third of its height. It is perforated by small square holes disposed like the geometrical figures — rhomboids. The fire burnt bricks of which it is built, have inscriptions on them, and so excellent is the cement that it is nearly impossible to extract a brick whole. The other parts of the summit of the hill are occupied by immense fragments of brick-work of no determinate figure, tumbled together and converted into solid vitrified masses, as if they had undergone the fiercest heat, or had been blown up by gun powder, the layers of brick being perfectly discern-

ible. These ruins stand on a prodigious
mound, the whole of which is itself in ruins,
channelled by the weather and strewed with
fragments of black stone, sand stone, and
marble."

Sir R. K. Porter has shown that the
intense vitrifying heat to which the summit
has evidently been subjected, must have
been the result of fire operating from above,
and was probably produced by lightning.
This is a curious circumstance taken in connection with the ancient Jewish tradition,
that the Tower of Babel was rent and over-
thrown by fire from heaven.

All authorities agree that it was thrown
down soon after it was built.

Porter thinks that the work of the
Babylonish Kings, especially the stupendous
temple of Belus, which was erected on the
site of the old tower, concealed for a while
the marks of destruction, and that now the
devastation of time and of man had reduced
it to nearly the same condition in which it
appeared after the destruction.

Mr. George Smith discovered the legend
of the building of the Tower of Babel

among the Assyrian tablets in the British
Museum, and gave an account of it in his
" Chaldean account of Genesis."

Heeren, in his "Asiatic Nations," says:
" There is, perhaps, no where else to be found
a narrative so venerable for its antiquity, or
so important in the history of civilization, in
which we have at once preserved the traces
of primeval international commerce, the first
political association, and the first erection of
permanent and secure dwellings."

There was something specially and signally displeasing to God in the building of
this tower. He commanded them to separate
and disperse in order that they should people
and cultivate the other parts of the habitable
earth. The attempt to settle permanently in
one place would, if successful, frustrate this
command. Pride, selfishness, and vain glory,
were the ruling motives that influenced the
confederacy; and whether idolatry had any
thing to do with this movement or not, it is
evident, that the spirit of true religion was
extinguished in the hearts of men, who delib-
erately adopted and persisted in a course of

action designed to defeat or defer the divine intentions, that they should, by occupying the earth, diffuse the knowledge of Divine truth and the blessings of civilization. According to the Divine plan, as we have just stated, men were to fill the earth — that is, spread over the whole earth; not, indeed, to live separately, but to maintain their inward unity notwithstanding their dispersion. The fact that they were afraid of dispersion is a proof that the inward spiritual bond of unity and fellowship, not only the oneness of their God and their worship, but also the unity of brotherly love, was already broken by sin. Consequently, the undertaking, dictated by pride, to preserve and consolidate, by outward means, the unity which was inwardly lost, could not be successful, but could only bring down the Judgment of Dispersion. The confusion of tongues led to this dispersion. The attempt at universal empire was completely put an end to by this extraordinary interference of God. The builders could not understand one another's speech. They were struck with awe at this manifestation of God's judgment which compelled

them to separate genealogically into separate
tribes and regions.

The confusion of tongues and the Dispersion form a remarkable epoch in the history
of the human race. It subsequently led to
the division of mankind into the two great
classes, the "Jews and Gentiles." It has also
given rise to a Masonic tradition, which is as
follows: The knowledge of the great truths
of God were known to Noah, and by him
communicated to his immediate descendants.
These preserved the true worship of God for
some time after the Flood; but when the
human race was dispersed, a portion of them
forgot this knowledge, fell into grievous
errors, and corrupted the purity of the truths
they received.

These truths were preserved in their purity
by a few in the patriarchal line, but still
fewer preserved only a part of the true light.
The first of these was confined to the direct
descendants of Noah, and the second was to
be found among the priests, philosophers,
and poets of the heathen nations and among
those whom they initiated into the secrets of
these truths.

The system of truths preserved and taught
by the former class has been classed by some
Masonic writers as "Primitive Freemasonry"
of antiquity, and the latter class as "Spurious Freemasonry" of the same time. Dr.
Oliver, the great Masonic historian, is the
first to use these terms, and applies them
thus: The "Pure Freemasonry" was that
which was taught by the immediate descendants of Noah in the Jewish line, and the
latter, or "Spurious," that which was taught
by his descendants in the Heathen or Gentile line. We shall treat of these divisions
more particularly as we proceed.

He says further "that it was at Babel that
this Spurious Freemasonry had its origin;
that is to say, the people there abandoned
the worship of the true God, and, by their
dispersion, lost all knowledge of His existence and of the principles of the truths upon
which Masonry is founded. Hence it is that
rituals speak of "the lofty tower of Babel as
the place where language was confounded
and Masonry lost."

We have here a beautiful and suggestive
symbolism. And it is only in this sense we

can receive it. The Tower of Babel represents the profane world of darkness and
ignorance. In contradistinction to this is
the threshing floor of Ornan, the Jebusite,
which represents Freemasonry, and is a symbol of it, because the Temple of Solomon, of
which it was the site, is the prototype of the
spiritual temple which Masons are building.
In this manner we can symbolically see how
that language was lost in the one and recovered in the other. We can, in like manner,
trace a Mason's advancement from his initiation to his "perfection," and see how his progress may be compared to that of truth from
the confusion of the Babel Builders to the
illumination of the Temple Builders, which
[Temple Builders all Freemasons are, and so
when, in the ritual, the Neophyte is asked
whence he comes and whither is he traveling, "From the lofty Tower of Babel where
language was confounded and Masonry lost
to the threshing floor of Ornan, the Jebusite, where language was restored and Masonry found."] On the above basis the
questions and answers become intelligible.
    We may here give an outline of what con-

stituted Spurious Freemasonry. The Bible distinctly points out that two races of men, very dissimilar in character, descended from Adam. These were the godly race of Seth and the ungodly race of Cain. The descendants of Seth, down to Noah, preserved the purity of the truth given them. This truth was embodied in legends and symbols which had been communicated to them by their common father, Adam. Cain and his posterity corrupted these or practically forgot them. Their wickedness at length brought on the destruction of the earth. They departed from the ways of God. Their Freemasonry was not the same as that preserved by the children and descendants of Seth. They changed the landmarks and corrupted and distorted the truths to suit their own wicked ends. For reasons set forth in the Bible, the two races, which had long kept apart, became united, and, as a consequence, the principles of the Pure, Primitive Freemasonry narrowed down to a very few individuals, so that, in the time of Noah, he and his sons were the only individuals who had preserved them in their original integrity.

These, with their families, were the only persons who had found favor in the sight of God, and on whom he had mercy.

Noah preserved the system pure, and of course, was the means of communicating it to the post-diluvian world. Thus, Primitive Freemasonry was preserved from Adam to Noah, and now after the deluge was the only system extant.

Through the perversity of the human heart this state of things did not continue. According to some chronologists, not longer than one hundred and forty years, according to others as long as nine hundred and twenty-five years. But chronology being a very uncertain science, we will not attempt to say which, in our opinion, is right; but we are cognizant of the fact that pure religion had greatly declined, and at the time of the "Dispersion" there was an open apostasy. This state of things was brought about by the wickedness of Ham, one of the sons of Noah, whom his father had cursed. Ham had been acquainted with the corrupt system of the Cainites, and gradually introduced it into the system of the Sethites. The cor-

rupt features of both systems were taught by
Ham. Now we have two parties professing
two different systems of Masonry; the one
preserving the great truths of religion, and,
consequently, of Masonry, which had been
handed down from Adam, Enoch, and Noah,
the other departing more and more from the
pure, original fountain. The dispersion at
the Tower of Babel appears to have been the
culminating point when there was an open
and irreconcilable schism. " The legends of
Freemasonry were altered, and its symbols
peverted to a false worship, the mysteries
were dedicated to the worship of false gods
and the practice of idolatrous rites, and in
the place of Pure or Primitive Freemasonry,
which continued to be cultivated among the
patriarchal descendants of Noah, was established those mysteries of Paganism, to which
Dr. Oliver has given the name of 'Spurious
Freemasonry.' "

Now the ritual of Freemasonry points to
the circumstance that the purity of its doctrine was lost to the greater portion of mankind at the confusion of tongues at Babel.
In one of the degrees of "Scottish Rite"

Masonry, this fact is referred to as the foundation of that particular degree. Two races of Masons are there distinctly named the Noachites, and the Hiramites. The first, as the name implies, conserved the Freemasonry of Noah and his descendants, and the latter were the descendants of Hiram. He was of the race of those who had inherited the Spurious Freemasonry. At the building of King Solomon's Temple, he was admitted into the Fraternity of those who had retained the truth. We shall further on treat of the "Mysteries" in which the doctrines of Spurious Freemasonry were embodied.

CHAPTER III.

The "Mysteries" of the ancient nations have been traditionally supposed to contain the doctrines of what has been designated as "Spurious Freemasonry."

In treating of these mysteries it would be highly interesting, if not specially important, if we could state positively *when* and *where* they had been originally instituted. We have no sufficient data, however, to enable us to fix with certainty the exact period of time or the country from whence they sprung. *India* and *Egypt* are mentioned as being the places where, in all probability, they had been first established. Undoubtedly, when mankind at the dispersion, had been separated into tribes and families, there were those to whom had been committed the special oversight of the preservation and conduct of their religious rites and ceremonies. From the nature of the case, these, who were so charged, paid more attention to

(34)

the knowledge, preservation, and performance of the religious practices than the
people in general.

They preserved, not alone their religious
ideas, but also they jealously retained and
guarded their habits, customs, and social
usages. Eventually, when they ceased their
migrations and nomad mode of life, and
settled themselves in permanent communities
in the different countries, there were developed three distinguishing classes among the
people, viz.: Priests, philosophers, and poets.
These retained, not only the *germs* but some
of the great fundamental truths of true
religion.

Although various changes are apparent in
the different mysteries, yet the scope and
design of them are singularly alike. From
this circumstance we are naturally led to the
conclusion that there must have been some
common source from which they were
derived.

The priests and philosophers of Egypt
and Phœnicia taught men as a public religion, that the sun, moon, and stars, were the
first eternal, and supreme gods. This idol-

atry, first set up by kings and ministers of
state, was everywhere the popular and political religion, at least, in great parts of Asia,
Africa, and Europe. But the secret doctrines taught in their " Mysteries " was, that
One Supreme Mind filled the whole universe
with his presence, power, and Providence;
and both formed and ·governed it. Also,
that the celestial luminaries, or gods residing
in them, were the subordinate ministers in
the Divine Providence in the several parts
of the world, and symbolically represented
the properties, perfections, and power of the
Supreme Deity. So that they thought the
Supreme Mind or God to be *all in all*, and ·
referred all the subordinate deities to him as
Supreme Head, and resolved their power and
ministerial government of the world unto
him as being the foundation of all being,
power, and perfection. Thus we see manifested in them a purity of doctrine which
clearly proves that they were the remnants
of a religion, once pure, but which subsequently became corrupted by mythological
rites.

The truths taught in these mysteries were

not known in the *popular* beliefs; for in all the ancient mysteries there were both an *esoteric* or secret, and an *exoteric*, or public mode of worshipping the gods. None but those who had been previously prepared by initiation were permitted to engage in the *secret* worship. |This secret worship was termed the " Mysteries.'|

Strabo, the historian, writing of them, says: "It was common both to the Greeks and to the barbarians to perform their religious ceremonies with the observance of a festival, and are sometimes celebrated publicly, and sometimes in mysterious secrecy."

Warburton, quoted by Dr. Mackey in his truly scholarly work, "Encyclopedia of Freemasonry," is authority for the statement, "That the most ancient of the mysteries of which we have any knowledge are those of Isis and Osiris in Egypt, for although those of Mithras came into Europe from Persia, they were, it is supposed, carried from Egypt by Zoroaster."

There were different degrees in these Mysteries. The candidate for each was subjected to a probation varying in length,

according to the degree to which he was to
be advanced. In some, the probation was
one year, in others, four, and in others much
longer. The death and resurrection of some
celebrated hero, or of some esteemed personage regarded as a god, were celebrated
in them.

It appears that the rites were practiced in
the darkness of the night, and often in the
gloomy recesses of the forest, or in subterranean caverns. The full measure of knowledge was not communicated until the candidate, severely tried, and thoroughly purified,
had reached the place of wisdom and of
light.

We may now ask what was the object of
establishing the " Mysteries? " Let us premise the answer to this question by remark-
ing, that there ever has been a propensity in
the human mind, to clothe in Mystery that
which it can not clearly elucidate. Bearing
this fact in mind, we can better and more
intelligently understand the object of the
establishment of these Mysteries.

Undoubtedly, it was the desire to establish an esoteric philosophy; that is, a phi-

losophy the secrets of which were to be concealed from the popular mind. It was supposed that the sublime truths contained in them, could only be intrusted to those who had been previously prepared for their reception.

A most probable supposition connected with them is, that the truths contained in the mysteries were communicated and transmitted by an ancient and highly civilized class of priests, who had their origin either in Egypt, or in the East, and that from them was derived religious and historical knowledge under the *Veil of Symbolism.*

The experience of human history demonstrates the fact that, even under the most favorable circumstances of civilization and enlightenment, religious and philosophical truths become corrupted by superstition and error. The history of Christianity itself evidences this fact. How, then, in the remote ages anterior to the institution of the Mysteries, was it possible to preserve truth from error, innovation, and corruption.

The following may somewhat elucidate the matter:

"The distinguished few who retained their fidelity uncontaminated by the contagion of evil example would soon be able to estimate the superior benefits of an isolated institution, which afforded the example of a select society, and kept at an unapproachable distance the profane scoffer, whose presence might pollute their pure devotions and social converse by unholy mirth and laughter."

We cite further, Plutarch, on the same subject, when he says: "It was a most ancient opinion derived as well by lawgivers as divines, that the world was not made by chance; neither did one cause govern all things without opposition." This quotation is taken from his "Isis and Osiris."

Again, quoting Warburton: "The Mysteries were at first retreats of sense and virtue, till time corrupted them."

Mackey says that a French writer, speaking of the origin of the initiations, places them at that remote period *when crime began first to appear upon earth*. His language is: "The vicious were urged by the terror of guilt to seek among the virtuous for intercessors with the Deity. The latter retiring

into solitude to avoid the contagion of growing corruption, devoted themselves to a life
of contemplation and the cultivation of several of the sciences. The periodical return
of the seasons, the revolution of the stars,
the production of the earth, and the various
phenomena of nature, studied with attention,
rendered them useful guides to men, both in
their pursuit of industry and in their social
duties. These recluse students invented certain signs to recall the remembrance of the
people, the times of their festivals and of
their rural labors, and hence the *origin of the
symbols and hieroglyphics* that were in use
among the priests of all nations. Having
now become guides and leaders of the people, these sages, in order to select as associates of their learned labors and sacred
functions only such as had sufficient merit
and capacity, they appointed strict courses
of trial and examination, and this must have
been the source of the initiations of antiquity.
The Magi, the Brahmans, the Druids, the
priests of Egypt lived thus in secluded habi-
tations and subterranean caves, and obtained
great reputation by their discoveries in

Astronomy, Chemistry, and Mechanics, by their purity of morals and by their knowledge of the science of legislation." He remarks further "that the first sages and legislators of antiquity were formed thus," and he thinks that "the doctrines taught in them were the Unity of God and the Immortality of the Soul, and that it was from these Mysteries, and their symbols and hieroglyphics, that the exuberant fancy of the Greeks drew much of their mythology."

Several writers give us the true nature and object of the Mysteries. Sophocles says: "Thrice happy they who descend to the shades below after having beheld these rites, for they alone have life in Hades, while all others suffer there every kind of evil."

Isocrates asserts, "Those who have been initiated in the Mysteries entertain better hopes both as to the end of life and the whole of futurity."

Plutarch, again says: "All the Mysteries refer to a future life and to the state of the soul after death," and addressing his wife says, "We have been instructed in the religious rites of Dionysus that the soul

is immortal, and that there is a future state
of existence."

. Plato, too, informs us "That the hymns
of Musæus which were sung in the Mysteries
celebrated the rewards and punishments
which await the wicked."

Modern writers also, among whom we may
mention Bunsen, gives a truly philosophic idea
of the nature of the Mysteries.   Dr. Mackey
quotes him as follows: "The religious
elements of the Mysteries consisted in the
relation of the Universe to the soul, more
especially after death.   Thus even without
philosophic proof, we are justified in assuming that the nature symbolism referring to
the Zodiac formed a mere frame work for the
doctrines relating to the soul and the ethical
theory of the Universe.   So, likewise, in the
Samothracian worship of the Kabiri the con-
test waged by the Orb of day was represented by the story of the three brothers
(the seasons of the year) one of whom is
continually slain by the other two, but ever
and anon rises to life again.   But here, too,
the beginning and end of the worship were
ethical.   A sort of confession was demanded

of the candidates before admission, and at
the close of the service the victorious god
(Dionysus) was displayed as the Lord of the
Spirit. The theorems of natural philosophy
did not form the subject matter of the Eleusinian Mysteries, of which, on the contrary,
the representation of natural objects were
the beginning and end. The predominating
idea of these conceptions was that of the
soul as a divine vital force, held captive here
on earth and sorely tried; but the initiated
were further taught to look forward to a final
redemption and blessedness for the good and
pious, and eternal torments after death for
the wicked and unjust."

We have before observed, that of all
the ancient mysteries of which we have
any knowledge, those of Osiris and Isis
are considered to be the most ancient.
Osiris was the chief god of the old heathen
Mythology. His worship was universal
throughout Egypt. He was the husband of
Isis. Various opinions are entertained by
different authorities as to who he was. One
opinion was that he represented the sun,
another that he was the god of the river

Nile. Another, again, is, that he represented the male and female productions of
nature. Whilst Osiris was the sun, his wife
Isis was the earth to be vivified by his rays;
and when he was represented as being
the Nile, the land of Egypt was Isis to be
refreshed and fertilized by his inundation.

He is said to be an historical character,
and as such to have been a powerful King of
Egypt who traveled over the world, leading
a numerous host after him. He taught and
civilized the whole earth, and taught mankind agriculture. The Symbolism of his
Mystery is his murder by Typhon, and the
recovery of his body by Isis and subsequent
rejoicings.

Typhon and Osiris represent the good
and evil principles which govern mankind.
The five pointed star, with one point upward
and with the sun or an eye in the center,
represents Osiris.

Herodotus, Pythagoras and Plutarch give
but a very short description of the Mysteries, although they had been initiates of
them.

Heredotus, especially shrank from any

exposure of them, either through fear of the consequences or because of his limited knowledge of them.

The church father, Clements of Alexandria, informs us, "that the more important secrets were not revealed even to all the priests, but to a select number of them only."

The suffering and death of Osiris and his resurrection were the great Mystery of the Egyptian religion. Combine with this idea the fact of his being a future judge, this surely points to the primeval revelation of the appearance of the Redeemer.

Whether we are to look to Egypt or not for the origin of the Mysteries, of one fact we are aware, that the Grecian rites were simply imitations of the Egyptians, and were never so impressively rendered.

The most important of the Mysteries were those of Osiris and Isis in Egypt, those of Mithras in Persia, of Cabiri in Thrace, of Adonis in Syria, of Dionysus and Eleusis in Greece, the Scandinavians among the Gothic Nations, the Driuds among the Celts, and the Samothracian.

The Eleusinian were the most sacred of

the Mysteries among the Greeks. It is thought that the Mysteries of Mithras had been transmitted from Egypt to Persia by Zoroaster.

Emblems, symbols, signs—features common to all secret associations — were employed in these Mysteries. It may be stated here that there is a strong probability, if not undoubted evidence, that the first learning of the world consisted of symbols, and that the wisdom of the Chaldeans, Phœnicians, Egyptians, and Persians was expressed and perpetuated in them, and, further, that they were not optional, but had been transmitted from antiquity and taught to the initiates like an alphabet.

The candidate for the Mysteries was required to give evidence of a purity of life. For several days previous to his admission, he was required to undergo different ablutions, confine himself to a particular dietry from which flesh meat was excluded. His conduct, too, was to be sacredly pure. The neighborhood of the great Pyramid of Cheops, near Memphis, seems to have been the center of this worship.

Naturally, then, it is to Egypt that Masons have always looked for the origin of the science of symbolism. Especially so, as they alone have preserved this peculiar mode of teaching. From Egypt the system of symbolism was transmitted to Greece and Rome and other countries, both in Asia and Europe, and through them down the ages, according to some authorities, "giving origin to that mysterious association which is now represented by the institution of Freemasonry."

An initiate of the Mystery of Isis, which was the first of the degrees (there being several) thus describes the ceremony: "The priest, all the profane being removed to a distance, taking hold of me by the hand, brought me into the inner recesses of the sanctuary itself, clothed in a new linen garment. Perhaps, curious reader, you may be eager to know what was then said and done to me. I would tell you, were it lawful for me to tell you; you should know it, if it were lawful for you to hear. But both the ears that heard these things and the tongue that told them would reap the evil results of their rashness. Still, however, kept in suspense, as you probably are, with religious longing, I will not torment you with long protracted anxiety. Hear, therefore, but believe what is the truth. *I approached the confines of death*, and having trod on the confines of Proserpine, I returned therefrom, being borne through all the elements. At midnight I saw the sun shining with its brilliant light, and I approached the presence of the gods above, and stood near and worshipped them. Behold! I have related to you things of which, though heard by you, you must necessarily remain ignorant."

In the whole range of the Ancient Mysteries, probably there is none that affords to the Masonic student such a field for investigation as that of the Mysteries of Mithras. It is presumed, with good reason, that it was introduced, as we have said, into Persia from Egypt by Zoroaster. Mithras was the chief of the twenty-eight second class divinities among the ancient Persian gods. He was the genius of the sun, and the ruling principle of the universe. Being " the supporter and protector of this life, he watches over the soul in the next, defending it against impure spirits, and transferring it into the realms of eternal bliss."

The Persians extended his worship into Europe, and it obtained such a hold there and lasted so long that traces of it have been found so late as the fourth century of our era. A certain writer, speaking of them, says: "With their penances and tests of the courage of the candidates for admission, they have been maintained by a constant tradition through the secret societies of the Middle Ages and the Rosicrucians down to the modern faint reflex of the latter — the Freemasons."

He was represented in the Ancient Symbols as a young man covered with a Phrygian garb and clothed in a mantle and tunic. He is kneeling upon an ox, one of whose horns he holds in his right hand and plunges a dagger into its neck. His birthday was on the 25th of December, and was kept as a special festival in his honor. The worship of Mithras was famous, and was universally spread over the whole Roman Empire. The ceremonies used in initiation were symbolic of the struggle existing between Ahriman and Ormuzd (the Good and Evil principle), and were of a very appalling character.

These Mysteries of Mithras were always celebrated in caverns. They were divided into seven degrees corresponding to the number of planets, and were: First, Soldiers; second, Lions (in the case of men) or Hyenas (in the case of women); third, Ravens; fourth, Degree of Persus; fifth, of Oromios; sixth, of Helios; seventh, of Fathers. This was the highest. It is thought his worship was introduced into Rome about the year 68 B. C., and was finally suppressed about the year A. D. 378.

The Church Father, Gregory Nazianzen, says that "no one could be initiated into the Mysteries of Mithras unless he had passed through all the trials, and proved himself passionless and pure."

The cult of Mithras ought to be considered at two different epochs; first, at its origin at the time of the Ancient Persian Monarchy, and, second, at the changes it underwent during the first four centuries of the Christian era. Traces of it were found to exist in the Semi-Pagan Gnostics. The Zend-Avesta are the sacred books of the Ancient Persians. The Mithraism found in it, as well as that found in the Roman monuments, would seem to indicate a mythological rather than an astronomical character. It appears that on the spread of the worship it lost its original character. Mithras was confounded with the sun and the Supreme Deity, and practices were adopted quite inconsistent with the Persian worship.

The fundamental dogma of the Mithraic doctrine was the transmigration of souls under the influence of the seven planets. After passing victoriously through the several ordeals, the Candidate was presented with an engraved stone or amulet as a token of his admission to the brotherhood and with the object of supplying him with the means of recognition by the brethren — its members. He was also offered a crown, which, however, he was instructed to refuse, saying, "My only crown is Mithras."

The followers of Mithras, we are informed, differing from the initiates of other systems, never wore wreaths, and when tried and proved as to their having been duly admitted to a participation in this mystery, throwing down the wreath offered them, say, "My crown is my God." The candidate, moreover, on the conclusion of his probation was *marked* in some indelible manner, the exact nature of which can not now be ascertained. We learn from sculptured tablets, and from inscriptions, and from symbols on tombs, that Mithraism prevailed extensively in England as well as in Germany; in each having been introduced by the Roman legions.

It is of the deepest importance as well as highly interesting to trace the spread of the human family, after the Deluge, from the Plain of Shinar, where they centralized. It was absolutely necessary that they should disperse from it. In time they had grown to be a numerous people, increasing to a vast multitude. With their flocks and herds the country had become too narrow for them. War or separation is forced on them. God ordained that it should be "Dispersion."

Following up one great branch of the human family we see that the first great wave of immigration, known as the Aryan, was across the great river, Indus, into India. The historians who treat of this subject tell us that they found already in India, a branch of the Turanean family who had already entered that country from the north and northeast. The Aryans entered by the southeast. It is to be presumed that wherever these went, they took with them their language, laws, customs, manners, traditions, and, certainly, their religious ideas.

Are we justified in supposing, that mankind at this remote period of his existence, was nothing but a mere savage or barbarian? By no means. Whilst the archæological discoveries of antiquity do not show that they were a highly civilized people, yet they exhibit abundant evidence that they were acquainted with many of the arts and sciences, of at all events, semi-civilized people.

And, what shall we say of their language? It has been generally the opinion that the oldest language of India was the Sanskrit. Philologists, however, tell us that there was an older still in which are *written* records

that are still extant. This fact, in itself,
diametrically opposes the supposition of a
barbarous or savage state of existence for
these people, even at this remote period of
antiquity.

We may here ask what antiquity can we
assign to the civilization of these people?
We know that Zoroaster is intimately connected with the civilization and religion of
the ancient Iranians, that is, of the Medes
and Persians. He was both a religious
reformer and a legislator among the ancient
Bactrians. Some critics deny that he was
an individual. They refer his name rather
to a period of time. Some apply the word
as a designation of a line of priesthood.
Assuming, as we do, that he was an individual; at what age of the world's history did
he appear? Conflicting opinions are entertained by different authorities respecting it.
It is very singular that there is a discrep-
ancy of some six thousand years between
the dates assigned by the different authorities — that is, between the earliest and the
latest. The earliest date given him is *six
thousand three hundred and forty-eight* years

before the Christian era; and the latest
authority places him *five hundred* years before that event.

The earliest Greek writer who mentions
him is Xanthius. He places him about
eighteen hundred years before Christ. Aristotle places him about six thousand years
before Christ. Berosus, the Babylonian historian, makes him a king of Babylon who
reigned about two thousand years before
Christ. And Dr. Haag, the author of
"Essays on the sacred language of the
Parsees" assigns him *one thousand years
before Christ*.

The late distinguished Mason, General
Albert Pike, says: "That in the Chaldean
lists of Berosus as found in the Armenian
lists of Eusebius (the Church historian), the
name Zoroaster appears as that of the
Median conqueror of Babylon, but he can
only have received his title from being a
follower of Zarathustra, and professing his
religion. He was preceded by a series of
eighty-four Median Kings, and the real
Zarathustra (Zoroaster) lived in Bactria
long before the tide of imigration had flowed

thence into Media.   Aristotle and Eudoxus, according to Pliny places Zarathustra (Zoroaster) six thousand years before the death of Plato.   Hermippus, five thousand years before the Trojan war.   Plato died three hundred and forty-eight years before Christ, so that the two dates substantially agree, making the date of Zarathustra's reign *six thousand three hundred*, or *six thousand three hundred and fifty;* and I have no doubt that this is not far from the truth."

Again, Bunsen, in his "God in History," places him not later than two thousand five hundred years B. C.   He styles him "One of the mightiest intellects and one of the greatest men of all times;" and that he was accounted by his contemporaries "a blasphemer, atheist, and firebrand, worthy of death, regarded even by his own adherents after some centuries as the founder of Magic; and regarded by others, as a sorcerer and deceiver."

Zoroaster lived in Bactria, a country on the north of Persia, situated between the River Oxus and the Caucasian Mountains. He denounced the nature worship of the old inhabitants, and established his spiritual religion, in which the antagonisms of light and darkness, of sunshine and storm, became transformed into antagonisms of good and evil, of powers exerting a beneficent or corrupting influence on the mind.

When we go to the Zend Avesta, the name of Zoroaster rises before us. His doctrine is a pure *Monetheism*. His conceptions of the Supreme Being are analogous to the Jewish conception of Jehovah. He calls Him "the Creator of the earthly and spiritual life, the Lord of the whole Universe, at whose hands are all the creatures."

God is regarded as wisdom and light; the source of all light, the rewarder of the virtuous, and the punisher of the wicked. He also teaches the doctrine of a future life; the immortality of the soul; heaven and hell; and in the Zend Avesta, the doctrine of the Resurrection is prominently taught.

A matter of special interest to Freemasons is that, in the Zend Avesta, sacred names are venerated in the same manner as among the Hebrews. One of these names signifies, "I am," and another, "I am who I am." This brings to our remembrance the sacred name announced by God to Moses when He said, "I am that I am."

We may conclude these remarks concerning Zoroaster by saying that in our opinion he lived about twelve hundred years B. C.— three hundred years after Moses; and that the sublime truths he taught, so singularly, yet so beautifully alike Divine Revelation, were obtained by him through not only the tradition preserved by his own people, but more especially from those derived from Balaam and others, who were contemporary with Moses. But from whatever source he obtained them, unquestionably he had been raised up providentially — and that to his eye of faith the external world was made apparent, and that some of the greatest thoughts that ever came from human lips, uninspired, came from him.

India, that magnificent land — a land of poetry and of beauty, of sunshine and of song. From its hoary past its ancient annals come before us. Its Vedas throw a flood of light on its ancient history and religion. They claim an antiquity of *four thousand years.* There is no doubt but that anciently Brahmanism taught a belief in a *Supreme Being*, and in the Immortality of the Soul. The primitive religion of India, in common with all ancient religions, was of a mystical character. Several writers have treated of it. Dr. Oliver, the great English Masonic writer, has collated the opinions of a number of them in reference to the ceremonies of initiations. Among these writers are Maurice, Colebrook, Jones, Faber, and others. In India, as in Egypt, the initiations were confined to the priesthood, In substance they were as follows: "The Deluge and the preservation of a patriarch with his three sons; Jyapti, or Lord of the earth, Charma, and Sharma. In one of the Vedas it is said that the *Royal* Patriarch loved Jyapti, and gave him the country north of India; but that he cursed Charma, because when the patriarch got drunk (unintentionally), Charma laughed at him, and in consequence, became a slave of slaves."

In this we have no difficulty in recognizing an allusion to the scriptural account of Noah and his three sons, Shem, Ham, and

Japhet. It appears that the ancient inhabitants, like the Bible patriarchs, practiced a patriarchal religion. In this system the head of the family was priest, prophet, and king, and offered up sacrifices, and also taught his people. We have no historical certainty *when* the Brahmanic worship was introduced. It consisted of two parts — rather was divided into two parts. It consisted of a Trinity: Brahma, Vishnu, and Siva. In one branch Vishnu was addressed who was represented as "Preserver." The other worshiped Siva, the "Destroyer."

We have already stated that the great truths of Revelation were preserved, though in the lapse of ages corrupted, in the great religious systems of antiquity. These Mysteries under contemplation, most assuredly, were a corruption of the original worship of the One God. They referred to the happiness and innocence of man in Eden, his transgression and destruction.

The ceremonies of initiation were performed in subterranean vaults, or caverns, hewn out of solid rock. (The principal of these was Elephanta near Bombay, said to be the oldest temple in the world constructed by man.] It is hewn out of a solid rock, and is estimated to be one hundred and thirty-five feet square, and supported by four massive pillars.]

The caverns of Salsette, also, are very remarkable. They are three hundred in number. They are also situated near Bombay. They have carved and emblematic characters. They are subdivided into compartments, which are connected by galleries. In the most secret compartments are placed the "ineffable symbols," which can only be approached by private entrances. They are so constructed as to have the highest possible effect on the mind of the candidate for initiation. A cubical "*sista*" for the burial of those who are initiated. This, too, was placed in the most secret recess of the cavern. In each cavern was placed the waters of absolution. The flowers of the lotus floated on the top. The periods of initiation were governed by the phases of the moon.

The Mysteries consisted of four degrees. A candidate was permitted to enter the first at the youthful age of eight years. The following significant language is used of them: "Let even the wretched man practice virtue *whenever he enjoys one of the three or four religious degrees;* let him be even minded with all created things; and that disposition will be the source of virtue."

"Corruption and reproduction" were represented as distinctly teaching the Resurrection. It was necessary for man to die, and his body to suffer corruption before it could be clothed with immortality by a Resurrection.

A lecture was given at the completion of the ceremonies. This related principally to the Unity and Trinity of the Godhead, the manner of using the sacred fire in the various religious rites. He is invested with a linen garment, and the sacred cord is wound round his head. The aspirant is now delivered to a Brahman who becomes his spiritual teacher and guide, and prepares him for many hardships, austerities, prayers and, ablutions for further advancement. He was to live a pure and most exemplary life; and was to be specially diligent in studying the sacred books that he might have a competent knowledge of the institutions, ceremonies, and traditions of the religion, which would qualify him for the next degree. Having attained a suitable age, and proficiency in knowledge, and attained a standard of fitness in other respects he was adjudged worthy of advancement to the next degree. In the probationary ceremonies of the second degree the austerities of the aspirant were increased. He supported himself by begging charity. Prayer, ablutions, and sacrifices occupied his days, and the study of the heavens his nights; and for necessary rest and repose from his arduous and almost exhausting duties, the first tree afforded him shelter; and after a short sleep, he arose to contemplate the constellations in the skies. In the hot season he sat exposed to five fires — four blazing around him, with the sun above. He stood uncovered, without a mantle, when the clouds poured the heaviest showers. In the cold season he wore no clothing, and went on increasing by degrees the austerity of his devotion. Having finished this probation he was admitted to the Mysteries.

The cross was marked on every part of his body, and he passed the probation of the Pastos or Coffin — which was called the door of Patala or hell — which was the Tartarus of the Grecian Mysteries.

Having finished all required preparations he was conducted to a subterranean cavern of gloom. *This was duly prepared for his reception.* It was brilliantly illuminated and showed with a splendor almost equal to that of the sun. The conductors of the ceremonies were magnificently dressed in rich and costly robes, *occupying the East, West and South*, representing Brahma, Vishnu, and Siva.

The aspirant was led into the midst of the assembly. He was then required to promise obedience to his superiors, to keep his body pure, to preserve inviolable secrecy on what was communicated to him on the subject of the Mysteries. He was then sprinkled with water, an invocation to Deity was whispered in his ear, he was then divested of his shoes, and made to circumambulate the cavern three times in imitation of the course of the sun; the officiating priest representing Brahma

stationed in the east, whose meridian height
was indicated by the representative of Siva in
the south, and whose setting by the representative of Vishnu in the West. He was
then conducted through seven ranges of dark
and gloomy caverns where the loss of Siva
was represented by dismal howlings. After
the performance of other ceremonies he
reached the end of the seventh cavern, and
was now prepared for enlightment by further
instruction and the administration of a
solemn oath.

The different ceremonies being concluded,
the sacred conch was blown, folding doors
were suddenly thrown open, the aspirant was
admitted into a spacious apartment filled with
dazzling light, ornamented with statues and
emblematic figures, decorated with gems,
and scented with the most sacred perfumes.

The aspirant was now supposed to be
regenerated, and was invested by the chief
Brahman with a white robe and tiara; a cross
was marked upon his forehead, and the *tau*
cross was marked upon his breast, and he
was instructed in the signs, tokens, and lectures of the Order. He was presented with

the sacred belt, the magical black stone, the
talismanic jewel to be worn upon his breast,
and the serpent stone which was to be an
antidote against the bite of serpents. And
last of all he was intrusted with the sacred
name. This was known only to the initiates.
This ineffable name was A. U. M. pronounced
Om, and is now usually written *aum*. It
could not be pronounced, but was to be the
subject of silent contemplation. The symbols and the *aporrheta*, or the sacred things
of the Mysteries, were now explained.

In concluding our notice of the Mysteries
we may mention that they continued to flour-
ish until long after the advent of Christianity.
In the fourth century the Christian religion
began signally to prevail, but the old established religion did not yield without a
struggle. The pagan priests, endeavoring to
make converts, threw open the very secrets
of their system. The lowest and vilest were
permitted to receive that which hitherto was
conferred only on the highest and noblest. At
length the corruptions and abominitions
became so intolerable that they were at first
partially suppressed by a decree of the two

Roman Emperors, Constantine and Gratian, and subsequently were wholly abolished by a decree of the Emperor Theodosius. This occurred in the year four hundred and eighty of the Christian era, and one thousand eight hundred years after their first establishment in Greece.

Thus far we have considered what has been styled "Spurious Freemasonry" and its development in the ancient "Mysteries" of the Gentile world. In these Mysteries we have presented to us the fact that man felt the impotency of his powers to reach the summit of his aspirations by himself. He yearned for something outside of himself— *he yearned for a Deliverer.*

This will be more fully entered into as we proceed to consider "Primitive Freemasonry" and its development in the Patriarchal line from Noah.

CHAPTER IV.

Dr. Oliver, before referred to, coined the word "Primitive Freemasonry." Its theory is that the principles of Masonry existed from the earliest dawn of man's history, and were practiced by him in his most primitive state. These principles were corrupted soon after the flood by Pagan priests and philosophers. They were, however, preserved by the descendants of Noah, and transmitted by them to succeeding ages. These principles, thus preserved, are distinguished by the name "Primitive Freemasonry," in contradistinction to the system embodied in the Pagan rites and called "Spurious Freemasonry." The ritual of Primitive Freemasonry, as it existed in the earliest ages of the world, must have been very simple. Its leading dogmas were the Unity of God, and the Immortality of the Soul. Oliver describes it thus: "It included a code of simple morals. It assured men that they who did well would be approved of God, and if they followed evil courses, sin would be imputed to them and they would thus become subject to punishment. It detailed the reasons why the seventh day was consecrated and set apart as a Sabbath, or day of rest, and showed why the bitter consequences of sin were visited upon our first parents as a practical lesson that it ought to be avoided. But the great object of this 'Primitive Freemasonry' was to preserve and cherish the promise of a Redeemer, who should provide a remedy for the evil that their transgression had introduced into the world when the appointed time should come." He expressed the opinion that the symbols and mysteries used were reduced to a regular system. The knowledge contained in the mysteries were imparted by God to Adam, and by him to Seth, and so on through the antediluvian patriarchs through Enoch to Noah, and then transmitted by them to Abraham, who communicated them to Isaac, Isaac to Jacob, and thus on to Solomon.

The above is an outline of the theory of Pure or Primitive Freemasonry, which has

descended with, of course, some modifications down the ages to the Freemasonry of
our own time.

"Thus far but no further" do we accept
of it, than that the truths of Revelation given
by God to man were conserved in their purity
in the line of the patriarchs as above out-
lined, and were but dimly shadowed forth in
the Pagan Mysteries, in which the original
truth was corrupted. This fixes the limit of
our acceptance of this theory. We have no
reason, and certainly no authority for believing that an organization analogous to Freemasonry existed among the patriarchs. We
delineate the subject more fully as follows:
It is for the glory and the highest well being
of man that in all ages of the world's history
great minds have been raised up, whose spirits
were consumed with the absorbing aim of
accomplishing a noble life-work. These are
the brave and lofty spirits who ever stood
forth as the uncompromising opponents of
wrong doing, and are the powerful factors in
the emancipation and ennobling of the race.
Men of great and rich natures, of large and
varied qualities of mind, displaying the

grand, moral heroism of the saint, armed
with righteousness and fearless intrepidity,
confronting with unblencing resolution a
hostile world; these build up an edifice in
whose higher ranges have ever been found
the noble army of martyrs, the poets, philosophers, prophets, and evangelists, the whole
array of moral magnates, who, most of all,
ennoble and enrich the race.

In the antediluvian period of man's history there stands prominently before us in
Bible history a truly religious and pious man,
Enoch, the seventh in descent from Adam.
"Enoch walked with God, and he was not,
for God took him." When we grasp the full
force of this comprehensive statement, we are
constrained to admit that no nobler por-
traiture of a man's character could possibly
be given. Meagre, indeed, is the account
given of him in Holy Writ. He was born
in the year of the world 622. His earthly
pilgrimage closed in the 365th year of his
life, by, as is generally taught, his translation
to heaven. "Enoch walked with God, and
he was not, for God took him." He is intimately connected with the traditions of

Freemasonry. *Enoch* means *to initiate and to instruct.* He is supposed to have been the first to unite religious teaching and human science. " It is thought probable that Enoch introduced the Speculative principles into the Masonic creed, and that he originated its exclusive character."

Of the early history of Enoch the Scripture tells us nothing. He probably dwelt near Mount Moriah. He was a prominent reformer of religion between the time of Seth and Noah. He appears to have been an instructor of his contemporaries in those rites and sciences with which he himself had been enlightened. Many traditions exist among Oriental writers respecting him. One tradition states that he received from God the gift of wisdom and knowledge. The Babylonians supposed him to have been intimately acquainted with the nature of the stars. There can be no doubt that he received direct from Adam the great facts of Revelation. The Greek Christians supposed him to have been the first to give instruction on the heavenly bodies, that he foretold the Deluge, built the Pyramids;

and ascribe to him the study of Astronomy.
A Jewish writer says that he was the first to
invent books and writing; that he discovered
the knowledge of the zodiac and the course
of the planets.

The Great Masonic tradition connected
with Enoch, is this: " Enoch, being inspired
by the Most High, and in commemoration of
a wonderful vision, built a temple under
ground and dedicated it to God.   His
son, Methuselah, constructed the building,
although he was not acquainted with his
father's motive. This building consisted of
nine brick vaults, situated perpendicularly
beneath each other, and communicating by
apertures left in the arch of each vault.

" Enoch then caused a triangular plate of
gold to be made, each side of which was a
cubit long, he enriched it with the most
precious stones, and encrusted the plate upon
a stone of agate of the same form. On the
plate he engraved, in ineffable characters,
the true name of Deity, and placing it on a
cubical pedestal of white marble, he deposited
the whole within the deepest arch."

" When this subterranean building was

completed, he made a door of stone, and
attaching it to a ring of iron, by which it
might be occasionally raised, he placed it
over the opening of the uppermost arch, and
so covered it over that the apperture could
not be discovered. Enoch himself, was not
permitted to enter it but once a year; and,
on the death of Enoch, Methuselah, and
Lamech, and the destruction of the world by
the Deluge, all knowledge of this temple,
and of the sacred treasure which it contained, was lost, until, in after times, it was
accidentally discovered by another, worthy
of Freemasonry, who, like Enoch, was
engaged in the erection of a temple on the
same spot.

"After Enoch had completed the subterranean temple, fearing that the principles of
those arts and sciences which he had cultivated with so much assiduity would be lost
in that general destruction of which he had
received a prophetic vision, he erected two
pillars — the one of marble to withstand the
influence of fire, and the other of brass to
resist the action of water. On the pillar of
brass he engraved the history of the crea-

tion, tne principles of the arts and sciences, and the doctrines of Speculative Masonry as they were practiced in his days; and, on the one on marble, he inscribed characters in hieroglyphics, importing that near the spot where they stood a precious treasure was deposited in a subterranean vault."

Josephus, in the first book of his Antiquities, gives an account of these pillars, somewhat similar to the above.

When Enoch had completed his work, we naturally suppose, he called his children and other descendants around him, and warned them of their sins and idolatries, and having exhorted them to return to the worship of the true God, he departed.

We desire here to draw the attention of the reader to the most interesting relic of antiquity — the " *Book of Enoch.*"

During the earliest ages of the Christian Church this book was well known, and stood among many in high repute.   A canonical writer in the New Testament quotes it.   At least it would seem so.   It has been the opinion in ancient and modern times that he did so.

We place the passage of both authors before you:

Apostle Jude, Epistle vs. 14, 15: "And Enoch also, the seventh from Adam, prophesied of these, saying: Behold the Lord cometh with ten thousands of his saints, to execute judgment upon all, and to convince all that are ungodly among them of their ungodly deeds, which they have committed, and of all their hard *speeches*, which ungodly sinners have spoken against them."

Enoch, Chapter II: "Behold he comes with ten thousands of his saints, to execute judgment upon them, and destroy the wicked, and reprove all the carnal, for everything which the sinful and ungodly have done and committed against him.

The Church Fathers, Irenaeus, Clement of Alexandria, Origin, and Hilary, all quote from the book, and say nothing which would go to show that any Christian of their day denied, or doubted but that the Apostle Jude quoted from it. Several writers, certainly, call in question the *canonical* authority of the book, but these, nevertheless, concede that the quotation in question was made by Jude.

After the time of Jerome, we find very little said about the book, until the eighth century, when Syncellus, a monk of Constantinople (about 790 A. D.), in a work entitled "*Chronography from Adam to Diocletian*," made large extracts from what he names *the first Book of Enoch.*

The last mention that is made of the Book of Enoch as extant and well known in former times, is that of Nicephorus, a patriarch of Constantinople, who flourished in the ninth century.

From the time of Nicephorus down to the period when Scalgier published an edition of Syncellus, nothing of consequence appears to have been either said or known respecting the Book of Enoch. Scalgier maintains that the Apostle Jude wrote it. Grotius, Walton, Heber, and many other writers spoke more or less respecting the book. At one time in Europe the deepest interest was manifested by the Literati respecting it. During a certain period in the seventeenth century, strong hopes were

entertained that the book had been discovered in the Ethiopic language, a feeling
existing at the time that the book was still
extant in Ethiopic. After repeated failures
to obtain it, all hopes of its recovery seem to
have died away. Many things were said,
many conjectures formed respecting it, but
it was generally supposed that it must be
ranked among the books irrecoverably lost.

At last, accident, almost, gave to Europe
what ages and generations had sought for in
vain. James Bruce, the well-known Abyssinian traveler, brought home with him the
long sought for *Book of Enoch*. It holds a
place in the Canon of the Abyssinian or
Ethiopic Scriptures, *and is arranged immediately before the book of Job*. Bruce brought
three copies of it. He presented one of
these to the Royal Library at Paris, another
to the Bodleian Library at Oxford, whilst he
reserved a third for his own use. Having
given this short *literary* sketch of the book,
we now proceed to give a very brief outline
of the contents of it.

He begins with apostate angels; and after
exhibiting their fall and punishment, he pro-

ceeds *to explain the Secrets of the Universe,*
as to the phenomena of winds, storms, heat,
cold, thunder, lightning, the motions of the
heavenly bodies, their changes and evolutions.
The *astronomical system* of the author is
next introduced, and dwelt upon through
eleven chapters. Then comes a chapter
respecting the Flood, and some prophetic
anticipations respecting it. Enoch then
addresses his descendants and exhorts them
to turn to the worship of the true God.

The author then proceeds: "All nature
obeys without transgressing the ordinances
of its Maker. The stars, the clouds, the
seasons, the trees, rivers, and seas, all obey
their appropriate laws. Only the wicked
disobey," etc.

We may mention that the work is divided
into one hundred and five chapters, full of
very curious matter. Chapters 51 to 71,
inclusive, are occupied with the author's
system of Astronomy or Astrology.

Only those persons who are deeply con-
versant with ancient Oriental astronomy can
intelligently understand this part of the
book. It is entitled "The Book of the

Revolutions of Luminaries of Heaven." For
the general reader this book of the luminaries is a sealed book, with the exception of
a few obvious facts.

When this book was written is a matter of
dispute. Different authorities assign different dates, varying from the time of the
Prophet Daniel, 600 years B. C., to the latter
part of the *first* century of the Christian
era. We recommend the reading of this
book to the Masonic student.

Another "Legend of the Craft" is found
in Noah. We know from the "Old Constitutions," that Noah and the flood are prominently mentioned in the work of the Craft.
He overlived the Deluge, and in him culmi-
nated all the knowledge of mankind through
the antediluvian patriarchs from Adam to
himself. As Masonry became developed the
Patriarch was adopted as a patron of the
Order. The connection of Noah with the
Masonic system was rendered closer because
many symbols borrowed from the "Arkite"
worship were introduced and incorporated
with the legends and traditions of Masonry.

The "Legend of the Craft" informs us

that "the three sons of Lamech, and his daughter Naamah, did know that God would take vengence on sin, either by fire or water, wherefore they wrote these sciences, which they had found in two pillars of stone, that they might be found after the flood."

"The first Masonic myth referring to Noah is one which tells us that whilst he was engaged in exhorting (the Sacred Historian calls him a preacher of Righteousness) his contemporaries to repentence, his attention had been often directed to the pillars which Enoch had erected on Mount Moriah. By diligent search he at length detected the entrance to the subterranean vault, and, on pursuing his inquiries, discovered the stone of foundation, although he was unable to comprehend the mystical characters there deposited. Leaving these, therefore, where he had found them, he simply took away the stone of foundation, on which they had been deposited, and placed it in the ark as a convenient altar."

Another myth preserved in Masonry informs us that the Ark was built of Cedars which grew on Mount Lebanon, and that

Noah employed the Sidonians to cut down
the trees under the superintendence of his
eldest son, Japhet.   Years after, when King
Solomon was building the Temple, the
descendants of these Sidonians were employed by him in felling the trees.

The account of Noah given in the Book of
Genesis lays the foundation for another of
these myths.   When Noah opened the win-
dow of the ark, that he might ascertain
whether the waters had subsided, he sent
forth a raven.   The raven did not return.
Then he sent forth a dove three different
times.   The second time she brought an
olive leaf in her mouth, a sign that the
waters were subsiding, and the third time
she did not return, a sign that the waters
were dried off the face of the earth.

The Arkite rites rose immediately after
the " Dispersion."   The dove was always
considered a sacred bird, in commemoration
of its use during the flood, being the first
discoverer of land.   In the Hebrew language
its name is *ionah.*   This name was given to
one of the earliest nations on the earth.   It
became the bird of Venus, because it was

considered an emblem of peace and good fortune.

Noah and his family remained in the Ark one year of 365 days. He entered it in the year of the world 1656. The circumstance of the number of the years of Enoch's life on earth, and the number of the days Noah remained in the Ark, were considered Mystic periods, so much so that the ancients paid idolatrous worship to the Patriarchs, who were saved from the Deluge. They were led also to become worshippers of the sun, because that as Noah was the restorer of the human race, he appeared to be, in some sense, a type of the regenerating power of the sun.

Every nation has a tradition of the Deluge. Naturally we may expect that it produced a profound impression on the religious thoughts and ceremonies of those people who succeeded to that event. In the traditional records, as well as the written documents of most nations and tribes, we will meet with the principle events connected with Noah and the flood preserved in greater or less purity. A reverential feeling would exist for such a personage in the minds of his descendants. From the person of the Chief, by a natural transition, the reverence would be transferred to that Ark which had preserved their great progenitor. The *Eternal One* — the preserver of Noah — would be worshipped in purity, whilst the traditionary circumstances would be circumscribed within its due limits. But at the confusion of tongues of Babel, and the dispersion of mankind therefrom, the true teachings of Enoch and Noah were lost, and idolatry and polytheism were substituted for the ancient faith. Noah, then, became a god under various designations, and worshipped accordingly. The Ark became a temple of the Deity. From these circumstances arose peculiar systems of initiation known by the name of "Arkite Rites." These formed a part of the religion of the ancient world in several of the countries.

/ Noah was six hundred years old when he entered the Ark. When he had come out of it he erected an altar to God and offered sacrifices of thanksgiving for his preservation. A Masonic tradition says that, for this purpose, he made use of that stone of founda-

tion which he had discovered in the subterranean vault of Enoch, and which, as we
have stated, he carried with him into the
Ark. At this time, God made his covenant
with Noah, and promised him that he would
never again destroy the world by a flood, and
he set his bow in the cloud in token of his
promise.

There is no evidence furnished us that
Noah ever removed from the neighborhood
of the place where the Ark rested. He lived
three hundred and fifty years after the flood,
and Oriental tradition tells us that he was
buried in Mesopotamia. His life, subsequent
to the Deluge, was spent in instructing his
descendants in the great truths of religion.
Hence, Freemasons are sometimes named
after him. As he was the repository of the
sublime and pure truths concerning God, so
they are, and have been through the ages,
the repositories and preservers of the sacred
truths of Masonry bequeathed to them from
their great ancestors. In the Ancient and
Accepted Scottish Rite Masonry, called
"Patriarch Noachite," there are certain circumstances recorded. connected with the

transactions of the immediate descendants of the great patriarch.

The primitive teachings of Noah must have been both simple and comprehensive. These truths continued to be preserved in the line of the patriarchs and prophets to the days of Solomon. They were, however, early corrupted and lost by the other descendants of the patriarch. They substituted for the worship of the One, true God, the worship of idols. Then, too, arose the "Arkite Rites," or the worship of Noah and the Ark, "Sabaism," or the adoration of the stars, and other superstitions. The priesthood, however, as we have before stated, preserved some of the great leading truths, in a greater or less degree of purity in their " Mysteries," and thereby formed a kind of Freemasonry, styled, " Spurious Freemasonry."

We now bring to view one of the most remarkable personages placed before us in either Sacred or secular history. Abraham, " the father of the faithful," and the " friend of God." He presents to us the most noble phases of character which we may well

conceive. A type of a true gentleman.
Courteous, affable, hospitable, and true to
friendship. Peaceable, yet a warrior chief.
A fearless upholder of the truths transmitted
to him.

Berosus, the Babylonian historian, says
that he was an eminent man among the
Chaldeans, and skilled in Celestial science.
He cites as his authority the Chaldean
records. Degeneracy and Idolatry made it
fit for God to raise up such a righteous man
as Abraham to oppose it, and to preserve the
knowledge and Spiritual worship of Him.
Josephus says he was the first who had the
courage to attempt a reformation of religion
after Noah. He was the fonnder of the
Hebrew Nation. In the degree of the
" Order of High Priesthood " Abraham is
personated. An interesting event in his life
gives rise to this. We may summarize the
Biblical account thus: On the peaceable
separation of Abraham and his nephew Lot,
the latter went to reside in the plains of
Sodom because of its fertility. There were
several cities in this plain governed by kings
or chiefs, and were subject to a king — Che-

dorlaomer — from whom they revolted. He
made war on them, and accompanied by
four other kings, invaded their cities, defeated them, took their goods and carried
away their inhabitants as captives. Lot was
among these. Abraham, hearing of this
circumstance, armed three hundred and
eighteen of his servants, and being joined
as confederates by Aner, Eschol, and Mamre,
pursued and defeated the invaders. He
rescued the prisoners and goods. Returning
from the slaughter of the kings, he was met
by Melchizedek, King of Salem, and a priest
of the Most High God, who refreshed
Abraham and his companions with bread
and wine. Melchizedek requested Abraham
to retain the goods taken, but Abraham
declined, saying, he had sworn an oath not
to keep even a "shoelatchet." This man
was to be "the father of many nations," and
in him were " all the families of the earth to
be blessed."

Isaac, his son, became the heir of the
promises made to him. He was the son of
the "freewoman," and Ismael was the son of
" bondwoman." According to some author-

ities, this constitutes a Masonic landmark, that none but those who are freeborn are admissible to initiation into the Fraternity.

Jacob and Esau were the two sons of Isaac. Jacob inherited the blessing. To him were the sacred truths more especially committed. One remarkable incident in his life, namely, his vision at Bethel, has been largely introduced into most of the "Mysteries." Jacob's ladder, a significant part of the Vision, occupies a prominent place in the Symbolism of Speculative Masonry.

This vision is recorded in the 28th chapter of the Book of Genesis. We outline it as follows: When Jacob obtained the blessing from his father, his elder brother, Esau, threatened to kill him. By the advice of his mother he went to sojourn with his uncle Laban in Padanaram. On his journey he lay down to sleep with a stone for a pillow, he had the vision of the ladder reaching from earth to heaven — "its foot on the earth, its top reaching to heaven." On this ladder he saw the angels of God *ascending and descending*. God promised to bless him, and give him a numerous posterity. When Jacob awoke he said: *"This is none other than the house of God, and the gate of heaven."* He consecrated the place to God.

This ladder occupies a remarkable place in the history of the Jewish people. It has also its place, as we have said, in almost all the ancient initiations. Why is it a common property of both? Is it from a mere coincidence, or is it derivable from a common source of symbolism? or, as the Masonic historian, Dr. Oliver suggests, is it that though the origin of the symbol was lost, yet the symbol itself was retained?

The philosophy of the Symbol exhibits advancement in moral and intellectual qualities of the mind, and is invariably represented by steps, gates, or degrees. The number, because of its mystical character, is seven.

Very beautifully does this Symbolism appear in the Persian rite of Mithras. In this Mystery was a ladder of seven rounds, which represented the soul's advancement to perfection. These rounds were called gates. The candidate was made to pass through seven winding caverns which were called

the ascent to the ladder of perfection. Each
was supposed to be an existence through
which the soul was to pass in his progress to
a higher state of being. The world of truth
was the final state.

In the Mysteries of Brahma there is also
an allusion made to the ladder of seven
steps. The Symbol was of the Universe.
The seven steps were emblems of the Indian
Universe. The lowest was the Earth; the
second, the World of Pre-existence; the
third, Heaven; the fourth, the Middle World,
or intermediate region between the lower
and upper worlds; the fifth, the World of
Births, in which souls are again born; the
sixth, the Mansion of the Blessed, and the
seventh, or topmost round, the Sphere of
Truth, and the abode of Brahma. The
Scandinavians, too, had a sacred tree which
denoted advancement from a lower to a
higher state of existence; from time to
eternity; from death to life.

In higher Masonry we find the ladder of
Kadosh, consisting of seven steps which
are, commencing from the bottom, Justice,
Equity, Kindness, Good Faith, Labor,

Patience, and Intelligence. Here we have the idea only of *intellectual* progress, yet that is carried to perfection by the topmost round, representing Wisdom or Understanding.

The Masonic ladder consists of three steps in its Symbolism, namely, Faith, Hope, Charity. "These enable us to advance in our Spiritual life from earth to heaven, from death to life, from mortality to immortality. Its foot is placed on the ground floor of the Lodge, which is typical of the world, and its top rests on the covering of the Lodge which is Symbolic of heaven."

In our galaxy of moral heroes we next come to consider the Man Moses. The meaning of the name is *drawn out*. He was the great law giver of the Jews. He is especially referred to in the Scottish Rite, in the Twenty-fifth degree, or Knight of the Brazen Serpent. Also in the Royal Arch of the York and American Rites; the Symbolism of these being entirely Mosaic. He was an actor in some of the most stupendous events that have occurred in the world's history. He stands before us as one of the

grandest characters in Scripture. To use
the language of the Sacred historian, "he
was brought up in all the learning of the
Egyptians." Behold him weeping as a help-
less babe in the Ark of bulrushes, placed on
the banks of the Nile. Forty years he led
a Shepherd's life, studying nature and
Nature's God. See him in the wilderness
by the bush that burned and was not consumed. Stand with him in the presence of
the tyrant Pharaoh — accompany him as
leader of the host of the Exodus — the lift-
ing up of the rod over the sea, his ascent up
the rugged hill of Sinai, his death on Mount
Pisgah with the Promised Land in view.
And who shall paint the grand moral heroism
of the man who laid down the sceptre, and
divesting himself, as it were, of the command
of a mighty nation, retired alone into the
dark defiles of the mountains, and there, in
its solitude, gave up his soul unto God —
and then, his mystic burial in a lonely vale
by the hand of the Eternal.

He was the founder of a magnificent
polity. He "spoke face to face with God."
How shall we connect him with Free-

masonry? We know that the religion
which God established on earth by him is
the most symbolic of any other religious
system of the world. In fact, types and
symbols were its main characteristics. We
may consider the *tabernacle* the center of
the religious symbolism. Everything connected with it, even to the vestments of the
attendants, was typical or symbolic. Ages
anterior to Pythagoras the mystical nature
of numbers had been inculcated by the
Jewish law giver. The *name* of the Eternal
God was couched in a symbolic form to
indicate his eternal, self-existing, nature.
When we examine the Mosaic Ritual as it is
delineated for us in the Pentateuch, especially
in Leviticus, we see that symbolism is the
pervading idea of it. The object in describ-
ing them with such minuteness of detail is,
"that the people might remember all the
commandments of the Lord and do them."

It is a grand fact, too, that in the Mosaic
worship there is not one single enactment
trifling or superfluous. To the Mason, the
Masonic Symbolism is of special beauty,
significance, and worth. From it the Ma-

sonic system has derived and transmitted
through its history some of its grandest and
most precious treasures of Symbolism.   Excepting in the higher degrees, everything in
the way of Symbolism possessed by the
Masonic Fraternity is derived from the
Mosaic religion.   For instance, the Symbol
of the Temple, everywhere employed in
Ancient Craft Masonry, is derived from the
Symbolism of the Tabernacle. /Solomon is
revered as the traditional Grand Master of
Freemasons. | He built the Temple which
was the Symbol of the Divine life to be inculcated in every heart.   The Temple, in a
sense, was but an enlargement of the Tabernacle.   The Jewish idea was, that every
Jew was to be a Tabernacle of the Lord.
Now,|the grand idea of Masonry is, that
every Mason is to be a Temple of the Grand
Architect.|

And   the   Christian   idea   embraces   and
transcends all. |*Your bodies are the temples
of the Holy Ghost.'| To the tabernacle then,
instituted in the wilderness, Ancient Craft
Masonry must look for its Symbolic teaching

(we would say almost exclusively), to the Tabernacle of the Wilderness.

We may here feel an interest in asking from whence did Moses derive the Symbolism which he introduced into his religious system? For an answer we have only to refer to the history of his life. "He was brought up in all the learning of the Egyptians," an obvious inference from which is "that he was instructed by the Egyptian priests in the philosophy of Symbols and hieroglyphics, as well as in the Mysteries of the sacred animals." Is it any wonder then, that when he became the leader of the Exodus, and led the people in the wilderness, and, under Divine guidance and inspiration, began to establish his religion, that he should have given a holy use to the Symbols which he had learned in the Egyptian Mysteries.

We need not be surprised then to find so much similarity existing between the Mosaic and Egyptian Symbols.

Some of the grandest truths that can possibly occupy the mind of man centre themselves around the Mosaic Dispensation. The most sublime and significant Masonic truth is comprehended in it. Let us consider the *Tetragrammaton*, or four-lettered name. "It is called the basis of our dogma and of our Mysteries." |It was forbidden to a Jew to pronounce it.| We know with what peculiar reverence the Masons regard it. It is the Ineffable or Unpronounceable name. In the sixth Chapter of Exodus, the sacred historian informs us, God said to Moses, " I am Jehovah; and I appeared unto Abraham, unto Isaac, and unto Jacob, as El Shadai (the Mighty One) but by my name Jehovah, was I not known." By this name it was now intimated that there would be a Revelation of the whole purpose of God — a manifestation of the Divine nature more fully than by any display of power, however glorious or irresistible. God in his character of Jehovah would fulfill the promises on which faith rested, and as such would be more fully recognized in the future.

The first consideration in connection with this name is, why was it *unlawful* to pronounce it. It is thought, at first sight, that it was because of a wish to conceal it from the surrounding heathen nations, lest they should desecrate it in their idolatrous practices. We know from Jewish writers that it was imperative that they should not pronounce it. One writer says "that name we are not allowed to pronounce. In its original meaning, it is conferred on no other being, and, therefore, we abstain from giving any explanation of it." Another says that the reason that the Holy Name was not to be pronounced " arose from a tradition based on the twenty-fourth chapter of Leviticus which was translated ' Whosoever shall pronounce the name Jehovah, shall suffer death.' "

In the third chapter of Exodus, when Moses asks God what is his name, replies, "*I am that I am.*" Say to the Children of Israel "*I am* that sent you." "This is my name forever." This is an expression of the name Jehovah, and is designed to show the personality, the self-existence and immutability of the Divine Being. In the historical development of the revealed relations of God to Man, there are two remarkable instances in which the name Jehovah (covenant God) is identified with Elohim (God)

viz.:   The covenant made with man, as mentioned in the second chapter of Genesis, and
the covenant here about to be entered into
with Israel.   The two ideas involved in the
name may be well combined as indicating
both the Unity of His Essence, and His love
for the Church, which He, Himself, designed.
He took these names in succession, to show
them that notwithstanding the lapse of time,
He was " always the same, yesterday, to-day,
and forever."

We are further informed " that the Knowledge of the Word was confined to the wise
men who communicated its true pronunciation and the Mysteries connected with it
only on the Sabbath day to such of their
disciples as were found worthy; but how it
was sounded was utterly unknown to the
people.   Once a year, on the great day
atonement, the holy name was pronounced
with the sound of its letters, and with the
utmost veneration by the High Priest, in the
Sanctuary.   The last priest who pronounced
it was Simeon the Just.   After the destruction of the City and the Temple at Jerusalem
by Vespasian, the true and genuine pro-

nunciation of the name was entirely lost to the Jewish people. Nor is it known how it was originally pronounced."

Jewish writers, themselves, doubt whether Jehovah was ever the true pronunciation. The idea prevails among them that when the Messiah comes he will reveal it.

In the Scottish Rite Masonry a tradition exists that the pronunciation was not always the same — that it varied according to the different ages in which the patriarchs lived — and that Enoch, Jacob, and Moses only knew how to pronounce it correctly.

The name, certainly, was known to the Patriarchs, before it was communicated to Moses, but with a different meaning. As it was communicated to Moses its essential meaning was *the Covenant God* — God very near in his relations to Man. And as a certain writer says: "That Moses in being initiated into the holy and comprehensive name of the Deity, obtains a superiority over the Patriarchs, who, although perhaps from the beginning, more believing than the long-wavering Moses, lived more in

the sphere of the innocent child-like obedience than of manly spiritual enlightenment."

What is the Masonic teaching in reference
to the Ineffable Name? It teaches that it is
the representative of the Word, and the
Word is the Symbol of the Nature of God;
and in Freemasonry, to know the Word is to
know the true nature and essence of the
Great Architect in all His attributes.

We next ask *when* was the pronunciation
of the word forbidden? Some are of opinion that it was made at the building of the
Second Temple. A Masonic tradition states
that it was discovered while the foundations
of the second temple were being laid. The
general opinion is, that it was in the time of
Moses the prohibition was laid. With this,
coincides the tradition of Freemasonry,
which holds that were it not for a certain
occurrence preventing it, it would have been
made known at the building of the first, or
Solomon's Temple.

The Ineffable Name of God is preserved
in Freemasonry, in an equilateral triangle
with the Hebrew letter, *Yod* in the centre.
In fact, both the letter G, and the Yod alone,

are recognized by them as Symbols of the Ineffable Name.

When was the name introduced into the ritualism of Freemasonry? As it is of the highest and deepest importance in the System; in fact, as it is the foundation principle of the whole, everything connected with it must be of the greatest importance to every Mason. Generally speaking, it is not of an esoteric character — that is, it is not of a secret nature in the Masonic system or symbolism.

We have no definite historical data to warrant us in fixing the exact time when the word was introduced into the Masonic ritual. Tradition alone, must be our guide. Certainly there are records in which allusions are made to it, but, as we have said, nothing certain or definite. Of one fact, however, we may rest perfectly assured, which is, that the *foundation* of Masonry, and the *use of the Word*, synchronise. The Hebrew Mysteries as well as the Masonic Symbolism, regard the Word, the True Word, or the Lost Word, as the Symbol of the Knowledge of the Divine Truth, or the true Nature of God.

From whatever source we trace Free-masonry we believe it is both a moral and an historical certainty that all along in its history the Word was the objective end of the whole system. From the records of the Mediæval Freemasons we know the Mystical use of the Word was employed among them. Their architectural emblems demonstrate this fact. Dr. Anderson plainly intimates in his " Defence of Masonry," written in 1730, that he was acquainted with it. His words are, " The occasion of the brethren searching so dilligently for their Master was, it seems, to receive from him the *Secret Word of Masonry*, which should be delivered down to their posterity in after ages."

It is highly interesting to Master Masons to bear in mind that up to the middle of the last century the holy name was given in the *third* degree and was styled the Master's Work, but was subsequently transferred to the Royal Arch. This was done by Dunckerly, an eminent Mason in England, who died in the year 1795, A. D.

Masonically considered, there centers around Solomon, the son of David, the great and wise King of Israel, a vast amount of historic and Symbolic material. He ascended the throne of Israel in the year 1015 before Christ, being then twenty years old. He was remarkable for his wisdom and knowledge. From the Bible we understand that the great object of his life and reign was the erection of a Temple to the worship of Jehovah. From this standpoint he is especially Masonically considered. Large preparations had been made by his father, David, for this building. He had all the workmen in his kingdom numbered. He appointed overseers of work, hewers of stone, bearers of burdens, and had prepared a great quantity of brass, and iron, and cedar, and had collected besides a large sum of gold, silver, and other treasures. David first conceived the idea of building the Temple. On consulting the prophet, Nathan, he was informed that though the project was pleasing to God, yet, as he was a man of many wars, he would

not be allowed to carry out the enterprise.
That honor was to be reserved for his son,
Solomon — the peaceful.

When David was about to die he expressly
charged Solomon to build the Temple when
he ascended the throne.   He also gave him
instructions relating to the construction of
the edifice, and gave him the money, amount-
ing to ten thousand talents of gold, and
twenty thousand talents of silver which he
had amassed towards the expenses.

Scarcely had Solomon become King, when
he began to make preparations for carrying
out the pious designs of his father.   In doing
this he sought the assistance of Hiram, King
of Tyre, who was both a friend and ally of
his father's.   The Tyrians had been distinguished builders and architects.   Many of
them were of a mystic building fraternity.
They were Dionysian artificers, and had long
monopolized the building profession of Asia
Minor.   The Jews were not remarkable for
their architectural skill.   King Solomon saw
the necessity of applying to Hiram for the
ьid of his skilled artificers, as he intended
the structure to be erected with magnificence

and splendor, and with as little delay as possible. He sent the following letter to Hiram:

"Know thou that my father would have built a Temple to God, but was hindered by wars and continual expeditions, for he did not leave off to overthrow his enemies till he made them all subject to tribute. But I give thanks to God for the peace I at present enjoy, and on that account I am at leisure, and design to build a house to God, for God foretold to my father that such a house should be built by me; wherefore I desire thee to send some of thy subjects with mine to Mount Lebanon, to cut down timber, for the Sidonians are more skillful than our people in cutting of wood. As for wages to hewers of wood, I will pay whatever price thou shalt determine."

Hiram replied to this letter in the following manner:

"It is fitting to bless God that he hath committed thy father's government to thee, who art a wise man endowed with all virtues. As for myself, I rejoice at the condition thou art in, and will be subservient to thee in all that thou sendest to me about, for when, by my subjects, I have cut down many and large trees of cedar and cypress wood, I will send them to sea, and will order my subjects to make floats of them, and to sail by what places soever of thy country thou shalt desire, and leave them there, after which thy subjects may carry them to Jerusalem. But do thou take care to procure us corn for this timber, which we stand in need of, because we inhabit in an island."

Hiram used all expedition in executing what he promised. We are told that he sent to Solomon thirty-five thousand and six hundred workmen of Tyre, besides enough timber and stone to construct the building. Hiram sent him also a far more important gift than either men or materials in the person of an able architect, "a curious and a cunning workman," who was to superintend the adorning and beautifying of the building. This personage was *Hiram Abif*, of whom we shall treat hereafter.

King Solomon commenced the erection of the building on Monday, the second day of the Hebrew month Tif, which answers to the

21st day of April, in the year before Christ
1012. Masonic tradition informs us that
Hiram the King, and Hiram the builder instructed Solomon in all the details of the
building of the temple, and that these three
constituted the first three Grand Masters of
the Craft, and arranged the workman in
order, saw to the payment of their wages,
and maintained that harmony which should
insure a speedy and satisfactory completion
of the work.

The general superintendence of the building was committed to Hiram Abiff, while to
other skilled artificers were committed the
oversight of different parts of the work.
These names and officers have been handed
down in the traditions of Freemasonry.

(The Temple was completed one thousand years before the Christian era./ It was
somewhat longer .than seven years 'in building.

The Bible further informs us that as soon
as the Temple was finished, King Solomon
made preparations for a solemn celebration
of the completion of the work. He directed
the Ark to be brought from the King's house

where it had been deposited by David. It
was deposited in the most impressive and
solemn manner in the Holy of Holies under-
neath the expanded wings of the Cherubim.
All who have received the Most Excellent
Master's Degree will remember how this
solemn event is commemorated in their
beautiful ritual.

The traditions of Masonry further inform
us that when the Temple was completed,
Solomon caused all the heads of the tribes,
the elders and chiefs of Israel, to assemble,
and to bring the Ark up out of Zion. To
the Levites was committed the care of the
Tabernacle. They accordingly delivered the
Ark of the Covenant to the priests, who
placed it in the center of the Holy of Holies.

Strictly speaking, with the completion and
dedication of the temple ends the personal
connection of Solomon with Freemasonry.
It is true that he had palaces and other
edifices built for himself in Jerusalem, and
further, our tradition tells us that he had
received as Most Excellent Masters those
worthy Masons who had been employed in
the building and completion of the Temple.

It would be well if we could end Solomon's life here at the completion of the wondrous and magnificent temple erected to the worship of Jehovah.

The after chapters of the great King's life are sad indeed. That noble mind so full of wisdom and magnanimity, so full of the Spirit of God, to become so clouded and perverted. To us it seems almost incomprehensible that he could have so fallen away as to consent to the erection of a temple devoted to idolatry, looking down on that edifice which he had so solemnly dedicated to the worship of Jehovah. Alas! for the perversity of the human mind. We believe, however, that Solomon became deeply repentant. He summed up the value of earth's attractions and pleasures in the comprehensive words: "Vanity of vanities! all is vanity."

In the whole records of Masonry, there is no personage, perhaps, on whose character and life we are so dependent on tradition as that of Hiram Abif. He is variously styled in the nomenclature of Freemasonry, "Hiram, the Builder," the "Widow's Son,"

and "Hiram Abiff." We find the earliest
account of him in the seventh Chapter of
Kings, where it is written: "And King
Solomon sent and fetched Hiram out of
Tyre. He was a widow's son of the tribe of
Naphtali, and his father was a man of Tyre,
a worker in brass, and he was filled with
wisdom and understanding, and cunning to
work all works in brass. And he came to
King Solomon and wrought all his work."

We find him again mentioned in the
Second Book of Chronicles in the letter of
King Hiram of Tyre to King Solomon.

"And now I have sent a cunning man,
endued with understanding, of Huram my
father's. The son of a woman of the
daughter's of Dan, and his father was a man
of Tyre, skillful to work in gold, and in
silver, in brass, in iron, in stone and in
timber, in purple, in blue and in fine linen,
and in crimson; also to grave any manner
of graving, and to find out every device
which shall be put to him, with thy cunning
men, and with the cunning men of my lord
David, thy father."

At this time the artists, architects, and

builders of Tyre were considered to be the most famous in the world. They excelled all others in mechanical skill. Hiram obtained this knowledge from his father. We presume his natural ability, quickened by diligent study, caused him to excel as an artist. At this time, Tyre was one of the principal seats of the Dionysiac Mysteries, which was a secret *operative organization* engaged exclusively as builders.

This secret organization of builders is thought to have been imitated by Operative Freemasons in later days. Probably Hiram was a member of this association. The regulation and discipline which Hiram found existing among the Dionysic builders, he introduced among the Jewish workmen, and thus formed a peculiar Organization of the Masons engaged in the building of Solomon's Temple.

Naturally, we would suppose, when the distinguished artist arrived in Jerusalem, he was received with every mark of respect by King Solomon, and admitted at once into his confidence. The superintendence of the whole building was committed to him. He received the title of " Principal Conductor of the Works." Before he came, this office had been filled by Adoniram. Masonic tradition tells us that Solomon, King of Israel, Hiram, King of Tyre, and Hiram Abiff formed the Supreme Council of Grand Masters. They arranged everything connected with the building of the Temple, and the government of the vast number of workmen engaged in it.

The tradition further states that as Hiram Abif was one of the Grand Masters, so in our Lodges he is always so designated. Tradition and Scripture both say that all the decorations and embelishments of the Temple were intrusted to him. He cast the two pillars of the Porch and the various metals that were to be used in the temple service.

The clay grounds extending between Succoth and Zaredatha was used by him for this purpose. He adorned the whole interior of the house from floor to ceiling. All were constructed of the most expensive timbers, and were overlaid with plates of burnished gold, and adorned with the most precious gems. The abundance of the jewels used in the decoration of the Temple is attributed to his agency. A tradition states "that about four years before the building of the Temple, he, as the agent of the Tyrian King, purchased some curious stones from an Arabian merchant, who told him upon inquiry, that they had been found by accident on an island in the Red Sea. By the permission of King Hiram, he investigated the truth of this report, and had the good fortune to discover many precious gems, and among the rest an abundance of the topaz. They were subsequently imported by the ships of Tyre for the service of King Solomon."

The temple was a work of stupendous undertaking; and we marvel at the character of the man who had the extraordinary ability to carry out the arrangements in detail without any confusion or discord. The stream of Masonic tradition uninterruptedly shows the wonderful genius of this personage. How, that every morning, with the utmost punctuality, he provided those immediately under him, and they to their subordinates, fresh designs, and thus the whole machinery of work and labor was carried on harmoniously.

The trestle board used by him in drawing

is said to have been made, as the ancient
tablets were, of wood, and covered with a
coating of wax. On this coating he inscribed
his plans with a pen or stylus of steel.

Another most interesting tradition symbolizing the faithful performance of duty is
preserved:

"It was the duty of Hiram Abif to superintend the workmen, and the reports of his
officers were always examined with the most
scrupulous exactness. At the opening of the
day, when the sun was rising in the east, it
was his constant custom, before the commencement of labor, to go into the Temple,
and offer up his prayers to Jehovah for a
blessing on the work, and in like manner
when the sun was setting in the west. And
after the labors of the day were closed, and
the workmen had left the Temple, he returned
his thanks to the Great Architect of the Universe for the harmonious protection of the
day. Not content with this devout expression of his feelings, he always went into the
temple at the hour of high twelve, when the
men were called off from labor to refreshment, to inspect the work, to draw fresh

designs upon the trestle-board, if such were
necessary, and to perform other scientific
labors — never forgetting to consecrate the
solemn duties by prayer. These religious
customs were faithfully performed for the
first six years in the secret recesses of his
Lodge, and for the last year in the precincts
of the most holy place."

The seven and one-half years required for
the completion of the Temple was drawing
to a close. The Fraternity was about to celebrate the cope-stone of the magnificent
structure with the greatest manifestations of
joy. But this joy was turned to mourning
in the sudden death of their Grand Master,
Hiram Abif. This occurrence filled the
Craft with the greatest grief, which was
shared in by his friend, King Solomon. In
the Book of Constitutions we read, "After
some time allowed to the Craft to vent their
sorrow, ordered his obsequies to be performed with great solemnity and decency,
and buried him in the Lodge near the Temple — according to the ancient usages among
Masons — and long mourned his loss."

We now give an outline of the history of

the Temple itself. It stood on Mount Moriah, on one of the ridges known as Mount Zion. This was originally, as the Bible informs us, the property of Ornan, the Jebusite, who used it as a threshing-floor. King David purchased it from him to build an altar there, it being the place where the "Angel of the Lord stayed the plague that was sent on the land because of his sin, in numbering the people." For the short space of thirty-three years it retained the splendor it had at its completion. Then it commenced to be given up to the hands of the spoiler. Shishak King of Egypt was the first who despoiled and carried away its choicest treasure. Ahaz desecrated it by the introduction of idolatrous worship into it. Manasseh, the son of Hezekiah, became professor of Sabianism, and set up an altar to the host of heaven. Nebuchadnezzar, King of Babylon, conquered the land, took Jerusalem, and utterly destroyed the temple, carrying the inhabitants away captive to Babylon. After the lapse of seventy years, they were restored.

The temple consisted of three divisions,

viz.: The porch, the Sanctuary, and the
Holy of Holies. It was surrounded with
extensive courts. The whole enclosure was
above half a mile in circumference. The
first court was the court of the Gentiles.
Next was the court of the Children of Israel
which was divided into two parts — the outer
one for the women — the inner for the men.
Here the Jews were accustomed to offer
their daily prayer. Within the court of the
Children of Israel, was the court of the
priests. The altar of burnt offerings was
placed in the centre of the court. Next
there is an ascent of twelve steps to the
temple proper, which, as we have said, was
divided into the porch, sanctuary, and holy
of holies. The Porch of the Temple was
twenty by twenty cubits in extent. A gate
made of Corinthian brass was placed at its
entrance. There were also two pillars
Jachin and Boaz which had been constructed
or molded by Hiram Abif. From this
porch there was access to the Sanctuary by
a portal. A magnificent veil of many colors
mystically representing the universe, separated these. The Sanctuary occupied one-

half of the body of the Temple. Here was
placed the altar of incense; the golden can-
dlesticks, and other necessaries for the daily
Service of the Temple.

Inside of all was the Holy of Holies, which
contained the Ark of the Covenant, which
had previously been kept in the tabernacle.
Into this most sacred place the high priest
alone entered but once a year — on the Great
Day of Atonement.

Viewing the Temple as a whole it must
present a magnificent spectacle. We may
summarize by saying that King David collected for its erection more than four thousand millions of dollars; and this besides the
vast amount expended by King Solomon
himself, and that eighty-four thousand six
hundred men were engaged in building it for
more than seven years. And after its completion it was most solemnly dedicated to
the worship of the Almighty, Who, to signify
His acceptance of the sacrifices that were
offered, sent fire from heaven to consume
them.

CHAPTER V.

We commenced at the fountain head of human history, and traced it from its source along its two streams or branches. The fountain was pure, but where the two streams branch or divide, a difference commences. The tendency of the one branch was to preserve its original purity, and of the other to corrupt itself. Very early in the history of the world, the human family became distinct and separate. One branch, the descendants of Seth, preserved the primeval revelation in its integrity; the other, the descendants of Cain, corrupted the truth. At the Deluge the latter branch was entirely cut off, and the fountain was once more pure. This, however, did not long continue, as Ham, one of the sons of Noah, again corrupted the truth. This corruption generally cumulating as the centuries passed on. But the truth was preserved in its purity all along the ages in the other branch.

Masonically speaking, were these streams ever again united? Yes, assuredly; they were blended in the persons of Hiram Abif and King Solomon, at the building of that glorious material temple — the Symbol of that Spiritual Temple. Yes, of that Temple, not made with hands, but Eternal in the Heavens.

These two personages united the two streams. They were the representatives of the two systems, the *"Spurious"* and the *"Pure and Primitive."* But again, the hand of death untimely cut off one of these, and the harmony which was established was once more disturbed.

We retrace our history somewhat. We ask the question, was there no intercommunication between the scattered descendants of Noah; was there complete isolation between the offspring of Shem, Ham and Japhet? We have abundant historical testimony to show that there was frequent communication between them. We know that Abraham sojourned in Egypt. But our important inquiry is, in all the history of the ages, was the "land of Ham" left without a testimony of the *Truth*, was there no record, no monument to attest to them, and to remind them of the Great Jehovah of their fathers? In this matter God certainly left them without excuse. "The invisible things of Him from the creation of the world are clearly seen, *being understood by the things that are made.*" "The Great, the Mighty God, the Lord of Hosts, is His name; great in counsel, and mighty in work, * * * which hast set signs and wonders in the Land of Egypt, even unto this day." Jeremiah 32, 18-20.

"The Great Pyramid, though *in* Egypt, is not *of* Egypt." This is that wondrous structure that was erected in the earliest ages of man upon earth, anterior to all Egyptian history, and centuries prior to the time when its use was perverted by Cainite pollutions.

"In that day shall there be an altar to the Lord in the midst of the Land of Egypt, and a pillar at the border thereof to the Lord."

"And it shall be for a sign and for a witness unto the Lord of Hosts in the Land of Egypt."

Egypt may be truly described as the land of Pyramids. By far the most ancient and immeasurably most important of these is the Great Pyramid, commonly known as the "Pyramid of Cheops." This structure stands not far from Cairo, near to, and in view of, the ancient Memphis. It is significant that the locality near this latter city is supposed to have been the centre of the worship of the ancient Egyptian Mysteries. Now this stupendous edifice is remarkable for the wonders of its internal structure, the mystery of its construction, and the *object* for which it was built. There is no doubt whatsoever of the object and uses of the other pyramids — they were used as sepulchres for the ancient distinguished Egyptian dead. Ascending, however, the stream of time, we find no Egyptian emblems or hieroglyphics in this, the most ancient of all the pyramids. Nor is there found a single vestige of heathenism, of idolatry, of sabaism, or of the worship of the sun, moon, or starry heavens.

Neither in the interior nor exterior of this "Great Pyramid," is to be found ancient Egyptian hieroglyphics of any kind.

Were the Pyramids built before the age of hieroglyphics? All authorities agree that they were not. How, then, can we account for the absence of those emblems which invariably characterize all Egyptian monuments? The answer is that though the Egyptians built this Pyramid, they were not the original designers of it. They seem to have obeyed some *compelling* and *constraining* power which prevented them placing any symbols of their corrupt form of worship on it. It is true that they afterward copied the Pyramid and used their own devised structures for the purposes of sepulture.

Various theories have been promulgated as to the object of building this Pyramid. These are. among others, a temple for the worship of the sun, moon, and stars — a burial place — an astronomical observatory— a place of resort in case of a second deluge, etc. All these theories are now clearly ascertained to be untenable, and as clearly does it appear that this grand, pre-historic monument was constructed on the facts of ancient Masonic conception, and its uses devoted to a lofty and sacred purpose.

But who were the mysterious persons who directed and superintended the construction of the great Pyramid, and to whom the Egyptians gave an unwilling obedience? The Egyptians ascribe to them every sort of abomination. They certainly were of a *different religious belief* to themselves. The answer will be understood as we proceed.

" When investigating the early history of the world the Hyksos cross our path like a mighty shadow, advancing from native seats to which is baffled the nations of antiquity to assign a position, covering for a season the shores of the Mediterranean Sea, and the Banks of the Nile with the terror of their arms, and the renown of their conquests, and at length vanishing with a mystery equal to that of their first appearance."

" It is monumentally proven that a most decided separation between the Old and New Empires of Ancient Egypt was caused by the domination of the " Shepherd Kings."

These " Shepherds " ruled Egypt rigorously with a rod of iron during the period of the 15th, 16th, and 17th dynasties, and as we may suppose considerably modified both the religion and architecture of the country.

But we must not, for an instant, suppose that these were the architects of the Great Pyramid. They lived too late in the world's history for that. *It* was built no later than the fourth dynasty, and the "Shepherds" who built it must have been contemporaneous with this fourth dynasty, and consequently were a totally different people.

The tide of emigration from the East kept pouring in all ages through the Isthmus of Suez into Egypt. We may therefore inquire whether at a period of time corresponding to the date of the fourth dynasty, or from one hundred to three hundred years before the time of Abraham there were any remarkable people who exercised governing power over the land of Egypt, and whether they were instrumental in building this Pyramid.

Manetho, who flourished about the year 270, B. C., makes a statement that the third dynasty was composed of Memphite Kings, and the fifth dynasty of Elephantine Kings.

The fourth dynasty is stated to be composed of "eight Memphite Kings of a *different race.*"

In the list of the early Kings of Egypt we have the following:

(1)   Soris reigned 29 years.

(2)   Suphus reigned 63 years.   He built the largest Pyramid, which Herodotus says was constructed by Cheops.   He was arrogant toward the gods, and wrote the sacred book; which is regarded by the Egyptians as a work of great importance.

(3)   Suphus II. reigned 66 years.

(4)   Mencheies reigned 63 years.

(5)   Rhatœses reigned 25 years.

(6)   Bicheres reigned 22 years.

(7)   Sebercheres reigned 7 years.

(8)   Thampthis reigned 9 years.

Altogether 284 years.

Egyptologists say they can confirm this by the monuments, by finding even in the great Pyramid itself, quarry marks (are they only quarry marks?) with two royal names which they interpret Shofo and Noumshofo, and say they are identical with the two Suphises mentioned in the list.

They say the first of these either built, or reigned during the building of the Great Pyramid.

What was his arrogance towards the gods? Evidently, the suppression of idolatrous worship.

We, again, quote Herodotus: "Cheops, on ascending the throne, plunged into all manner of wickedness. He closed the temples and forbade the Egyptians to offer sacrifice, compelling them instead to labor one and all in his service; that is, in building the Great Pyramid."

"Cheops reigned fifty years, and was succeeded by his brother Chephern, who imitated the conduct of his brother, and built a temple — but smaller than his predecessors, and reigned fifty-six years.

Thus, during 106 years the temples were shut and never opened.

"After Chephern, Mycerinus, son of Cheops, ascended the throne. He re-opened the temples, and allowed the people to resume the practice of sacrifice. He, too, built a Pyramid, but much inferior in size to his father's. It is built for half of its

height, of the stone of Ethiopia. That is
expensive red granite."

"After Mycerinus, Aoychis ascended the
throne. He built the eastern gate of the
Temple of Vulcan, and being desirous of
eclipsing all his predecessors on the throne,
left as a monument of his reign a pyramid of
brick."

Now we have here four Kings, each building a temple. Two of them are commended
and two are execrated. Why? Those two
who are execrated, and who built the earliest
and largest of the Pyramids discountenanced
idolatrous worship, and the others threw the
temples open for such abominations. It was
not, therefore, *because of erecting the Pyramids* in itself that they were so hated, but
because they acted as above stated.

Herodotus further says: The Egyptians
so detest the memory of these (two first)
Kings (Cheops and Chephern) that they do
not much like even to mention their names.
Hence they commonly call the Pyramids
(the Great and the Second) after Philition or
(Philitis) the "Shepherd," who, at that time,
fed his flock about the place."

Here, certainly, we have a very significant fact. A stranger in Egypt, a Shepherd-prince, distinguished in connection with the greatest of the monuments of that country, and who certainly was not one of the Hyksos of the comparatively recent, but totally different persons, as we have already said, to those who appeared as the "Shepherd Kings" in the 15th, 16th, and 17th dynasties.

Rawlinson admits that he was a Shepherd-prince from Palestine, and conjectures that he was so powerful and domineering that it was the *traditions* of *his* oppression in that early age that filled the Egyptians with such religious, bitter hatred against the Shepherds' oppression of the latter dynasty.

"One of the priests writes: "We had formerly a King whose name was Timeus. In his time it came to pass, I know not how, that God was displeased with us, and there came up from the East, in a strange manner, men of an ignoble race, who had the confidence to invade our country, and easily subdued it by their power without a battle."

As we have stated, King Shofo reigned at this time. Is it not then most probable that prince Philitis was enabled to exert a certain amount of control over him and his Egyptian subjects, and not by *military conquest* either, but by some powerful, we will say, supernatural influence over their minds.

Further, Manetho says, they quitted Egypt to the number of 240,000 people, and went to Judea and built there a city of sufficient size to contain this multitude of men, and named it Jerusalem.

It would appear then that this Prince, Philitis, after having long controlled King Shofo during the time that the Great Pyramid was building, left Egypt with all his people and flocks, proceeded to Judea, and built a city which he named Jerusalem.

Who was this remarkable personage who appeared so early in the world's history, and assisted at the building of the Great Pyramid? Be it remembered that according to the most generally received dates the Great Pyramid was erected in the year 2170 B. C., and must, as we have said, considerably antedate the time of the Patriarch Abraham.

Now, very little is said in the Bible respecting Melchizedek, King of Salem, and priest of the Most High God, to whom Abraham paid tythes. Some consider Salem to have been Jerusalem.

Can it be then that, that grandly mysterious kingly character, Melchizedek, was the individual?

It is true that the Bible gives no account of any special mission of this man to Egypt, neither does it say anything of his early life. There must be a direct allusion in that passage of the second Chapter of Deuteronomy where Moses encourages the Israelites in their march under God's favor and guidance, out of Egypt and Palestine, by mentioning two other but long preceding occasions on which God had shown similar favor to other people, and they were established successfully.

First "the children of Esau, and afterwards the Caphtorim, which came forth out of Caphtor." This Caphtor is generally considered to have been Egypt. In fact, Lower Egypt, or Pyramid Egypt. By Caphtorims is not necessarily meant native Egyptians. The term may apply to sojourners there.

It must be distinctly borne in mind that there is no evidence whatever to show that these ancient Egyptians, prior to the erection of the Great Pyramid, had any architectural knowledge by which they would have been capable of erecting such a building as the Great Pyramid. It burst suddenly on this ancient world. There it stands since for upwards of 4,000 years. It is truly an unique structure. Though situated in Egypt, yet, in no sense, corresponding in scope or design to the religious life of a people given wholly to idolatry, and consequent rebellion to the Eternal Jehovah.

Those buildings that are of a purely Egyptian character are emblazoned with sculpture, pictorial designs, and hieroglyphics. Yet the Great Pyramid is markedly free from any such, excepting quarry marks.

Here I would state that *the stones required were, evidently from the quarry marks and instructions still legible upon some of them, prepared at the quarries according to the architect's orders a long time beforehand.*

Again, no absolutely certain date can be

assigned for the erection of the character-
istically Egyptian built structures, but
astronomical science fixes to a certainty the
building of the Great Pyramid.

Another significant fact, too, may be mentioned in connection with it. All the other
buildings as soon as they were built, sub-
served their purpose, for either worship or
sepulture. Not so the Great Pyramid. No
such use was ever made of it. The theory
of the Coffer or Sarcophagus is now exploded,
for by actual measurement it has been ascertained that it was too large for any of the
openings on the lower part of the first
ascending passage.

The grand design for which it was built
in the early ages of the world, could no
more be set aside, than the destruction of
Solomon's Temple, and the carrying away of
its sacred vessels to be used in the idolatrous
worship of the Babylonians, could prevent
the fulfillment of the Hebrew prophecies
touching their chief end, viz.: the appearance of the Saviour of mankind among the
Jews at Jerusalem.

That great end for which it was designed

was to perpetuate in stone (which is more imperishable and reliable than manuscript), a proof to men of the existence of a Supreme Being, the One Eternal God, the Supreme Architect of the Universe, and to show that He interferes by His Providence in the affairs of men; and also to show that there would be a fulfillment of the promise of the Messiah, the Saviour of mankind.

This is not expressed in any language, but is conveyed in terms of scientific fact, so as to make its lesson, when properly understood, universally known to mankind.

We can here state that the subjects of the Fourth Dynasty's Egyptian King were the *actual builders.* This King was called Cheops in Greek, and Shofs in Coptic. But the *designer* of the building is Philitis in Greek, and Shem or Melchizedek in Scripture.

We have the Scripture statement that "every Shepherd is an abomination to the Egyptians." If we seek the explanation of this we must go back to the struggle between Cain and Abel. Abel had faith in the Divinely appointed means of sacrifice as

pre-figuring the atonement of the Mediator.
This was rejected by Cain and his descend-
ants, and this rejection was perpetuated by
Ham and his descendants after the flood;
and all ethnologists agree in classing the
Egyptians as Hamites. In the rejection of
God's appointed sacrifices, the Egyptians
were certainly Cainites. We can, therefore,
understand the great opposition of the
Egyptians to the building of the Great
Pyramid. They were compelled to erect a
non-idolatrous monument.

The intelligent Freemason will at once see
the significance and importance of the foregoing as well as the following.

Here we have a building coming forth
suddenly in primeval history, "having a
numerical knowledge of grand, cosmical
phenomena of both earth and heaven." It
is built into the level surface of the solid
rock. Two casing stones have been found
in their original positions demonstrating
what was the real outside finishing of the
building. It was smooth, polished, white
limestone, exhibiting matchless workmanship
as correct and as true as optical work of the

modern instrument makers.   But the marvel
is that the precision here is exhibited on
blocks 5 feet high, 8 feet broad, and 12 feet
in length, with joints and cement in the
interstices no thicker than silver paper!

Further, it sets the true scientifiic rule of
orienting its sides to the true cardinal points,
and this in contradistinction to the temples
erected at Thebes and Nubia which have no
regard to Orientation, and which were used
for idolatrous purposes; and to the Chaldean
temples in Mesopotamia, which had their
sides placed at an angle of 45° from any
cardinal point, and which were glaringly
dedicated to the false gods.

The symbolic and scientific design of this
grand structure could never, at that age of
the world, have been intentionally arrived at,
without being guided by a mighty intelligence both superhuman and supernatural.

A traveler writes of them thus: "To
view them merely as gigantic monuments is
a novelty productive of impressions of sublime grandeur, of which words fail to convey
any accurate conception, but when they are
viewed in connection with the history of the

human race, as older than the oldest records,
and marked with the antiquity of those ages
long gone by when the earliest of the patriarchs entered Egypt, the mind becomes
absorbed, and I felt as though I could have
lain, not for hours only, but even for nights,
indulging in the Light of the greatest of
these Pyramids."

We know that it is specially since the
revival of learning in Europe that the
supremely important Mathematical problem
of what has been familiarly known as
"Squaring the Circle," had taken such hold
on the human mind. This is no wonder, as it
forms the basis alike of practical mechanics
and astronomy, and the form π, or the proportion of the diameter to the circumference
of a circle, is found to be one of the most
wonderful and necessary results of the
growth of science for all ages and degrees of
intellectual men; and that, too, in an increasing proportion as they arrive at a high state
of civilization, material progress, and practical development.

It is a remarkable fact that the entire
structure of the Great Pyramid should give

the earliest numerical value to the world, by
making up this one grand, mathematical
figure, the true value of π, or 3. 1415 + &c.—
and that none of the other (thirty-seven)
pyramids indicate this great fact.

Were we to follow out the various details
and facts connected with this wondrous
structure, we would see that in its entirety
it is Symbolical in design, scientific in detail,
and exhibits the greatest possible mathematical accuracy throughout its whole structure.

Thus far we have traced the existence of
Truth through the only three sources possible to us, viz.: The Primeval Revelation
of God to Man handed down to us from
Adam through the patriarchs, in the line of
Seth in the antediluvian period, and through
Shem in the post-diluvian period. The mon-
umental witness of the truth perpetuated in
the Great Pyramid, and such portion of the
truth as was preserved in the "Ancient
Mysteries."

CHAPTER VI.

We now inquire what is Freemasonry? Is it a religion? If so, what are its tenets?

Dr. Oliver describes it as "a system of morality by the practice of which its members may advance their spiritual interest, and mount, by the theological ladder, from the lodge on earth to the lodge in heaven. Freemasonry, however, is not a system of religion. It is but the handmaid to religion, although it largely and effectually illustrates one great branch of it, which is practice." In the English Lectures it is described thus: "Freemasonry is a beautiful system of morality, veiled in allegory, and illustrated by symbols."

Dr. Mackey, to use his own words, gives "a more comprehensive and exact definition of it" when he describes it as "*a science which is engaged in the search after Divine Truth, and which employs symbolism as its method of instruction.*

The principles of Freemasonry are, assuredly, religious. It embraces the leading features of religion. To say that it is not a religious institution would be to deny its fundamental principles. It has been founded and nurtured in religion, and it is to its preeminently religious character that it owes its development. Hence, any endeavor to separate Freemasonry and religion would be to destroy the foundation principles of the Order.

What do we understand by religion? Lexicographers tell us that " Religion consists in a belief in the existence and perfections of God — in a Revelation of His will to man — in man's accountability to Him — in his responsibility to obey His commands, in a state of rewards and punishments — in true godliness and piety of life — and in the practice of all moral duties to God and our fellow-men in obedience to His will."

Generally speaking, religion is defined to be " any system of faith or worship." In this sense, of course, it includes Mohammedans and Pagans as well as Christians.

Therefore we speak of different systems of religion

/ It is a *landmark* in Freemasonry that no atheist can be made a Mason./ At the very threshold, before any of the ceremonies of initiation are gone through, he is required openly and solemnly to declare his trust in God. The Revelation of God's will to man is technically called "the spiritual, moral, and Masonic trestle-board" of every Mason. By these he is to erect a spiritual temple to eternal life. True godliness and piety of life is inculcated on every Mason as the rule of his conduct. The voice of the Grand Architect of the Universe speaks to us through the symbolism of every ceremony from the very inception of the candidate into the Order.

These symbolisms and ceremonies speak to every true Mason commanding him to fear God and to love the brethren. The very statutes of the Order owe their sanction to the Masonic tenets of the nature and perfection of God; and these have come down to us from the earliest history of the Institution.

The whole object of Freemasonry was the preservation and promulgation of them.

Certainly, as we have said, Freemasonry is not a *system* of religion. As touching the religious belief of any man, we do not make the distinction that he is a Christian, a Jew, a Mohammedan, or a Mason as indicating a particular system of religious belief. We have already said that Masonry teaches religious truths; but because it is a religious Institution, it must not on that account be confounded with, nor assume the place of Christianity, as a religion. We emphatically deny that it is offered *as a substitute* for Christian obligation and duty. Neither does it make any attempt to supersede it, nor any other form of religious belief. It does not, in any sense, interfere with sectarian creeds or doctrines, but it teaches fundamental religious truths. It is not incompatible with the Christian Scheme of Salvation, nor does it do away with it, but in its whole scope, and in its true spirit, the Christian will find in its types and ceremonies, everything to lead his thoughts to the contemplation of the most sublime teaching of his own inspired faith.

When we look at its ancient landmarks, its symbolism, its rites, its ceremonies, its profound allegories, we see that the tendency of true Masonry is toward religion. The religious spirit of the Institution is the motive power of its development and progress. A true devotional spirit pervades the whole of its forms. The blessing of God is solemnly invoked both in the opening and closing of the Lodge. The holy law of God is appealed to, and is exhibited openly on all altars. A spirit of reverence and humility is inculcated towards the Great Being we worship. Of course, a man may be truly religious without being a Mason, but we do claim most emphatically, that every Mason, *true to the principles of his Order*, must be a respector of, and must be guided by, the principles of religion.

The religious principles of Freemasonry, do not make it sectarian in its nature. No man is rejected because of his peculiar religious tenets, and no man is accepted because of them. It inculcates virtue, and points to righteousness, and its whole tendency is Christian. We again emphasize the statement that it is not a substitute for Christianity.

Freemasonry, however, has a creed, which is very simple in its form. Without assent to this no man can be received into the order. This creed consists of two articles, viz.: 1st. A belief in God, the Creator of all things, visible and invisible, who is recognized as the Great Architect of the Universe. 2d. A belief in the Resurrection to Eternal Life — this life being probationary and preparatory to it. In this, of course, is included the immortality of the soul. Assent to the first of these is implicitly required of every candidate before initiation, and the other is impressively taught by the legends and Symbols, especially of the Third Degree. Every Master Mason knows that that degree is founded on the doctrine of the Resurrection unto life.

(The whole design of Freemasonry, both in its religious and philosophical aspect, is the search after Truth. / The other features of the system are incidental and subordinate. The peculiar phase of the Truth, is the Unity of God, and the Immortality of the Soul.

The different degrees are emblematic of the various stages of the human mind, and the difficulties under which it labors in its progress from the darkness of ignorance to the light of Truth. This Truth is symbolized by the *Word*. From the first inception of the Apprentice's degree to the attainment of the last, this search is continuous. The end of all his labors, the Symbols explained, the ceremonies used, tend to the one object — the attainment of the Truth.

In the Masonic system Truth has two meanings or applications. In the Lecture of the First Degree, Truth and Sincerity are identical. "Brotherly Love, Relief, and Truth" are spoken of as the "three great tenets of a Freemason's profession." Truth here is called a "divine attribute, the foundation of every virtue," and is synonymous with honesty of purpose. The other, and higher idea of Truth is that which underlies the whole Masonic system, and which is symbolized by the *Word*, and is that which refers to the highest conception of God.

In Operative Masonry, whatever uses may have been assigned to the Word, in Specula-

tive Masonry, the Word is, as above expressed, symbolic of the Truth, and the
search for it is the whole object of Freemasonry. It is the foundation of the whole
system. Nor can it be altered without un-
dermining the whole fabric of the institution.

When *specially* referred, the Word is used
in connection with the *Third Degree*. Certainly there is a secret word in each degree.
As we have already seen, the use of a word
is of great antiquity, as they were used in
the ancient mysteries.

The philosophy of the Word is seen in the
mythical history of Freemasonry. This informs us that there was once a WORD of ex-
ceeding great value, and of the profoundest
veneration which was known only to a few.
It was at length lost. A temporary substitute, however, was adopted. The philosophy
of Masonry teaches us that there can be no
death without a resurrection, and we see in
nature, that there is no decay without a subsequent restoration — on the same principle
it follows that the loss of the Word must
simply be its recovery.

This is exactly the myth of the Lost Word

and the search for it.   It is immaterial how,
when, or in what manner it was lost, nor yet
when or in what manner it was recovered,
nor why a substitute was provided.   These
are of secondary importance.   The legendary
history, it is true, depends on them, but not
the understanding of the symbolism.   The
abstract idea underlying the myth is a word
lost and recovered.   In the interpretation of
this consists the philosophy of its teaching.

The Word is the symbol of *Divine Truth.*
The loss, the substitution, and the recovery,
are simply parts of the mythical symbol representing the search after Truth.   These
symbolize the decay, corruption, and loss of
pure religion among the nations of antiquity
after the Dispersion of Mankind from the
plain of Shinar, and of the efforts of the wise
men, priests, and philosophers to find, retain,
and perpetuate it in Secret Mysteries.

Independently of this, there is a particular
or individual interpretation of it.   In this
interpretation the Word and its accompany-
ing myth of a loss, a substitute, and a recovery symbolizes the progress of the candidate from his initiation until he receives the

highest degree, when the full blaze of the
Sublime truths of Masonry illuminates his
whole mind.

Thus then, the Apprentice begins in seek-
ing for the light which is symbolized by the
Word. As a fellow Craft he continues this
search, still asking for more light. The
Master Mason does not get it, but he gets a
substitute. Why? The True Word, the
Divine Truth, does not dwell in the first
temple of this, our earthly pilgrimage, it can
only be found in the second temple not made
with hands, and is eternal in the heavens.

Some may be curious to know the qualifications necessary for admission into the
Fraternity of Freemasons. There are, as we
would naturally suppose, certain essential
conditions required. The qualifications are
of two kinds. *Internal* and *External*. The
internal are those which are known only to
the individual himself. They lie concealed
in his own bosom. The external refer to his
outward and apparent fitness. The external
are subdivided into *Moral, Religious, Physical, Mental,* and *Political*.

I.   The *Internal* qualifications are:

1st. The applicant must come of his own free will and accord, that is, his application must be purely voluntary.

2d. He must not be influenced by mercenary motives.

3d. He must be led to make application for admission to the Order in consequence of a pre-conceived favorable opinion of it.

4th. He must be willing to conform to the usages of the Fraternity.

II. (1st.) *Moral* qualifications. No candidate is qualified for initiation unless he observes faithfully the moral law, leads a virtuous life, and so orders his whole behavior that he has the testimony of his own conscience that he walks blameless before God and man.

2d. *Religious*. Every candidate is required to believe in the existence of God, as a superintending and protecting power, to whom he is accountable for his acts. Also in a future life.

3d. *Physical*. These refer to age, sex,

and bodily soundness. The candidate must be a man, of mature age, and must be in possession of all his limbs.

4th. *Mental.* The candidate must have sufficient mental capacity to understand the nature of the Institution.

5th. *Political.* This refers to their social standing; that is, that they must be free born, and not in slavery.

This seems essential, because, as Freemasonry involves a solemn contract, no one can reasonably or legally bind himself to the performance of it unless he is a free agent and his own master to do so.

Being admitted into the Fraternity his instruction commences. In fact, at a very early period in his initiation, he is taught that the great tenets of Freemasonry are *Brotherly Love, Relief, and Truth.* And at every step of his progress this is repeated so as to impress indelibly on his mind the necessity of the practice of these virtues, and also to constantly remind him that they are stereotyped in the whole constitution of Freemasonry.

We may, indeed, naturally suppose that
in such an organization as Freemasonry,
Brotherly Love would become a distinguishing feature. Nor is this sentiment inculcated as a mere abstraction. Neither is it
left indifferently to be practiced or violated
at the will of the member according to his
own individual feelings of selfishness or gen-
erosity. It is very particularly defined, its
practice is clearly set forth and illustrated
by Symbols so that there is no room left for
indifference. His duty is plainly set forth,
and no apology is left for indifference to, or
violation of, Brotherly Love.

This is more particularly described in
what is technically known as the "Five
Points of Fellowship," so called from their
allusion, symbolically, to certain parts of the
human body.

Several Masonic writers represent these
as —

1st. "When the necessities of a brother
call for my aid and support, I will be ever
ready to lend him such assistance, to save
him from sinking, as may not be detrimental

to myself or connections, if I find him worthy thereof.

2d. "Indolence shall not cause my foot-steps to halt, nor wrath turn them aside, but forgetting every selfish consideration, I will be ever swift of foot to serve, help and exe-cute benevolence to a fellow creature in distress, and more particularly to a brother Mason.

3d. "When I offer up my ejaculations to Almighty God, a brother's welfare I will remember as my own, for as the voices of babes and sucklings ascend to the Throne of Grace, so most assuredly will the breathings of a fervent heart arise to the mansions of bliss, as our prayers are required of each other.

4th. "A brother's secrets delivered to me as such I will keep as my own; as betraying that trust might be doing him the greatest injury he could sustain in this mortal life; nay, it would be like the villainy of an assassin who lurks in darkness to stab his adversary when unarmed and least prepared to meet an enemy.

5th. " A brother's character I will support in his absence as I would in his presence.   I will not wrongfully revile him myself, nor will I suffer it to be done by others if in my power to prevent it."

Every aspirant, before admission into the Masonic Brotherhood must enter into a covenant to observe certain regulations and usages of the Order.

A covenant is a contract between two parties.   Every Mason enters into a contract with the institution.   He binds himself to perform certain duties and to observe certain obligations.   The Fraternity engages to reciprocate this by a covenant of friendship, protection and support.   In the different degrees there are different covenants.   The covenant of an Entered Apprentice is different from that of a Fellow Craft and that of a Master Mason from either.   As the applicant advances in Masonry the obligations increase, but this does not annul any of the preceding ones.

The covenant in Masonry is symbolized by the most essential and necessary of all the ceremonies of the Institution.   In fact it is the foundation stone on which is erected the whole superstructure. From the nature of the case, it is the covenant that makes the Mason.

As the covenant is of special importance in establishing the relationship between the Mason and the Fraternity, it follows that the contract must be attended by the most solemn and binding ceremonies. This is analogous to the solemn manner of entering into and observing covenants both among the Hebrew and other nations. In the fifteenth chapter of the Book of Genesis we have the first mention of *the Form* a solemn covenant of a religious character. This was when Abraham, in obedience to God's command, took a heifer, a she goat, and a ram, "and divided them in the midst, and laid each piece one against another." This denoted the covenant between Abraham and God.

An Institution founded on the belief in One, Personal God, must, in all its work and undertakings acknowledge Him as the giver of all things. He must be invoked for blessings and for guidance. Prayer is one of the characteristics of Freemasonry. All its work is opened and closed with prayer. We shall not enter here into the theological aspect of prayer, but we will say that prayer is a necessity of the human soul.

The custom of commencing and ending labor with prayer was adopted very early in the history of the Operative Masonry of England. Findel, in his history of them, says: "Their lodges were opened at sunrise, the Master taking his station in the East, and the brethren forming a half-circle around him. After prayer, each craftsman had his daily work pointed out to him, and received his instructions. At sunset they again assembled after labor, prayers were offered, and their wages paid to them."

The following is a form of prayer used in the reign of Edward the Fourth (at the initiation of a brother Mason) from 1461 to 1483:

"The might of God the Father, of heaven, with the wisdom of his glorious Son, through the goodness of the Holy Ghost, that hath been three persons in One Godhead, be with us at our beginning, give us grace to govern in our living here, that we may come to his bliss that shall never have an end."

CHAPTER VII.

There are two branches or divisions of Masonry, viz.: OPERATIVE and SPECULATIVE. Thus it is treated both as an art and a science. In the Middle Ages the Operative part was practiced by the Stone Freemasons of Germany. The Speculative part is that which is practiced by the Freemasons of the present time.

Every person knows what Masonry, as an operative art is. It is engaged in the erection of buildings for public or private purposes, according to the plans or designs of architecture. Of course it has technical terms applicable to its art, and uses various implements peculiar to itself. Speculative Masonry, founded on Operative Masonry, employs the technical terms, usages, implements, etc., of Operative Masonry.

Before we enter directly on a consideration of the Speculative division of Freemasonry, we promise by saying that in Specu-

lative Masonry there are what are called
Symbolic Degrees. Further on we shall explain what these are, and why so called.
There are lectures given in these Degrees
which instruct the neophyte in the difference
between the Operative Art, and the Speculative Science of Freemasonry, and the distinction between them is familiar to all Masons.

Speculative Freemasonry is an intellectual
development from the Operative. At one
time both were united. From this we must
not understand that there ever was a time
when every Operative Mason was acquainted
with the *Speculative* aspects of the art. We
know that there are thousands of the most
skillful artisans of the present day who know
nothing whatever of the Speculative Aspects
of the Science. But Operative Masonry was
the initial of Speculative Masonry. It was
the Statue without life, until the *Speculative*
breathed into it a life which energized it.

Speculative Masonry, and Freemasonry as
we now understand the term, are identical.
We will here quote Dr. Mackey's definition
of Speculative Masonry: " It is the scientific
application and the religious consecration of

rules and principles, the language, the implements, and the materials of Operative
Freemasonry, to the veneration of God, the
purification of the heart, and the inculcation
of the dogmas of a religious philosophy."

In the application of this definition we
must consider Speculative Masonry as an
ethical system, having its distinctive doctrines.

We may consider these under the three-
fold division of *Moral, Religious*, and *Philosophical*.

1st. *Moral* Doctrines. "A Mason," the
old charges say, "is obliged by his tenure to
obey the moral law." This moral law is to
its fullest extent of conception embraced in
the Decalogue of Moses, commonly called
the "Ten Commandments." The "law of
nature" is too indefinite. The universality
of the moral obligation of the Institution of
Freemasonry is, as we say, to the fullest extent comprehended in the Decalogue. Because every thought, word, and act, of every
human being, is a violation or observance,
consciously or unconsciously, of the negative
and positive demands of that "Law of

Moses," more correctly, *that Law of God*. Freemasonry is a social institution, and much of its moral character arises from, and is dependent on, its aspect as such. It is, we know, "an association of men bound together by a common tie," and therefore in its very first stage it is necessary that in its teachings, obligations of kindness and man's duty to his neighbor should be inculcated. The Charge to the Entered Apprentice says: "There are three great duties, which, as a Mason, you are charged to inculcate — to God, to your neighbor, and to yourself." And your duty is that we should do unto others as we would wish they should do unto us.

The express object of Freemasonry is to practically carry out, to their fullest extent those lessons of mutual love, and mutual aid, that are such essential features of a Brotherhood. The socialism of Freemasonry, like that of Christianity, has a high ideal. "It is a community of sentiment, of principle, and of design, which gives to Masonry all its social and hence its moral character."

The moral design of Freemasonry in its

social aspect, is to make men better to each
other, to cultivate brotherly love, and to perpetuate and practice those social and moral
virtues which pre-eminently characterize our
Brotherhood. /The keystone of all moral
duty is the precept of our Divine Master,
the wondrous GOLDEN RULE, "*Do unto others
as we wish they should do unto us,*" On this
is founded the practice of active benevolence,
"relieve the distressed, visit the sick and
afflicted, give good counsel to the erring,
speak well of the absent, observe temperance
in the indulgence of appetite, bear evil with
fortitude, be prudent in life and conversa-
tion, dispense justice to all men." These
duties are specially and prominently placed
before the candidate and impressed on his
mind in the most solemn manner, as obligatory duties of the Order.

In all the history of Freemasonry — in its
operative character, before the speculative
element became its prevailing feature — the
old Constitutions of the Craft teach us that
this moral element was enforced on its members. In the Records of the 15th, 16th and
17th centuries, we have the following, viz.:

That "Masons shall be true, each one to the other; that is to say, to every Mason of the science of Masonry that are of Masons allowed, ye shall do to them, as ye would that they should do unto you."

RELIGIOUS DOCTRINE. We have already treated of the religious element in Masonry. We will here repeat that its Creed is very simple and self-evident. It is belief in God, and the Immortality of the soul. No man can be a Mason and deny these, for the whole of the Symbolism of "Symbolic Masonry" distinctly and emphatically teach them, and they terminate by revealing the awful Symbol of a life after death, and an entrance upon immortality.

The moral phase of Masonry, in its highest sense, can not exist apart from its religious. The moral and religious elements are based upon each other, or rather they are mutually dependent. Before we can rightly estimate and truly appreciate the Universal Brotherhood of Man, we must recognize and realize; that is, we must KNOW AND FEEL the Universality of the Fatherhood of God.

In the Old Records already alluded to, we

see the religious spirit manifested in the
Masonry of the Middle Ages. The ancient
Constitutions always begin with an invocation to the Holy Trinity, and sometimes to
the Saints. The charges which were published in the year 1723, and which was a
compilation from those older records, declare
that whilst a Mason is left to his own peculiar views in religious matters, he is required to believe in God, and an eternal life.

PHILOSOPHICAL DOCTRINES. These are
not, generally, so well understood as the
moral and religious phases of Masonry. They
are, however, of special importance to every
member of the Craft. The Philosophical
truths underlying the whole system of Masonry are different from either the moral or
religious.

The objects of the religious and moral elements are to make men virtuous, whilst the
philosophical are designed to make them
zealous Masons. The more we devote ourselves to the study and contemplation of our
Noble Craft — the more we see the depth of
the philosophy embraced in its symbolism —
the more we apply ourselves to the contem-

plation of the sublime truths hidden in these symbolisms — the more faithful, the more earnest, and the more zealous Masons we will become. If we know nothing of the significance of the philosophy of our Order, we shall in time lose that interest which should ever characterize those who obligate themselves in the solemn manner Freemasons do. We shall grow lukewarm and indifferent. But if we study these things, the more we study, the greater the beauty we shall behold, and the more ardor, enthusiasm, and faithfulness we shall manifest. The philosophical truths of Masonry are developed from the symbolic teaching which especially characterize its whole system. "These relate to lost and recovered word, the search after Divine Truth, the manner and time of its recovery, and the reward that awaits the faithful and successful searcher. It brings us into close relation to the profound thought of the ancient world, and makes us familiar with every subject of mental science that lies within the grasp of human intellect."

We see then, that the moral, religious, and philosophical truths underlying the whole system of Freemasonry, relate to the social, the intellectual, and the eternal welfare of man.

In this connection we may say, that whilst the Operative Institution, which gave rise to the Speculative, inculcated moral and religious truths, there was no reference made to philosophical teaching.

We have abundant proof to show that the Operative Masons were acquainted with the Science of Symbolism, but we have no proof that they employed them, to any great extent, at least, to explain moral and religious principles. There is but little doubt that the philosophical doctrines are a development of Speculative Masonry.

We have repeatedly mentioned the term *Symbolism of Masonry.* What do we mean by the expression? It is that science by which we investigate the meaning of symbols, and by which we apply the interpretation of them to religious, moral, and philosophical teaching.

In Freemasonry there are three Symbolic Degrees. These are the Entered Apprentice, Fellow Craft, and Master Mason. The term is not applied to the higher degrees. It is exclusively confined by way of distinction to the above three degrees, and is of constant and universal application.

It can not be too emphatically stated that the germ of all Masonry lies in these three degrees. All the others are emanations from, or developments of, them. At one time in the history of Masonry they were the only degrees known to the Craft. When so recognized and practiced they included the Royal Arch. From the circumstance of their being the original degrees they are appropriately styled "Ancient Craft Masonry" to distinguish them from the comparatively modern additions which are commonly known and designated as the "Higher Degrees." The peculiar feature of these primitive degrees is, that their essential mode of instruction is by symbols. Of course, they have their legends, to; indeed, they have many of them; for example, the building of the Temple, the construction of the pillars of the porch, and the payment of the wages in the Middle Chamber. These, however, constitute no very special feature of the degrees.

The lessons imparted to the candidate are, principally, through the medium of symbols, whilst there is very little traditional teaching, excepting the great legend of Masonry, the "GOLDEN LEGEND" of the Order. This is found in the Master's Degree, and is a symbol of a most solemn, profound, and abstruse nature. The details of the legends, most interesting in themselves, are but subordinate features of the great symbol. Hiram the Builder, is the representative, in profound Symbol, of Manhood laboring for immortality. And it is this symbol of the MASTER WORKMAN that gives it its spiritual life, and imparts its true meaning and significance.

Because Symbolism is the prevailing characteristic of these primitive degrees, and because the science, the philosophy, and the religion of Ancient Craft Masonry is concealed from the profane, or uninitiated, and imparted only to the initiated that they are said to be Symbolic.

Symbolism is not wanting in the higher degrees, but it is *legend* and not Symbol, that constitutes their main feature. The legends themselves are, undoubtedly, Symbolic, but they do not, as in the primitive degrees of Masonry, "Strike the eye, inform the mind, and teach the heart, in every part of the Lodge, and in every part of the ceremonial initiation." In other words, in the higher degrees, as historical legends form their chief features, so Symbolic instruction does not constitute their predominating characteristic, as it does of the first three degrees.

The Masonry taught in these degrees is most appropriately designated Symbolic Masonry, and the Lodge in which this Masonry is taught is known as a *Symbolic Lodge*.

In Freemasonry each degree is a system of development. Development is an *unrolling or unfolding*, from the Latin word *devolvere*, to unroll or unfold. From this we get the English words *to develop*. The idea derived from this etymology is appropriately applied to the development of Freemasonry. The ancients, writing their books on parchment, made them up into a roll. From this we get the word *volume*. This word is derived from *volvere*, "to roll up." In the two

words we have the act of "rolling" and
"unrolling" conveyed to our minds. The
system of SPECULATIVE MASONRY is a
volume folded from unlawful eyes, and the
person who desires to understand its deep
and true meaning, its sublime teaching, its
significant symbols, must commence at the
beginning, and "read, mark, learn, and
inwardly digest" the lofty truths it presents.
The deep knowledge contained in the system
can only be attained and developed therefrom
by laborious and continued research.

"The student must begin as an Apprentice
by studying the rudiments that are unfolded
on its first page. Then as a Fellow Craft
still more of the precious writing is unrolled,
and he acquires new ideas. As a Master, he
continues the operation and possesses himself of additional material for thought. But
it is not until the entire volume lies unrolled
before him in the highest degree, and the
whole speculative system of its philosophy
is lying outspread before him, that he can
pretend to claim a thorough comprehension
of its plan. It is then only he has solved the
problem, and can exclaim, "the end has

crowned the work." Thus can we realize
that Masonry is a scheme of development.
Certainly, he who looks only on the cover,
no matter how attractive or ornamental it
may be, can learn nothing of the design or
spirit of the volume. Leaving the figurative
and coming to the realistic, we again repeat,
that the true Mason will not neglect the
unrolling of the parchment, but will be constantly adding to his stock of Masonic ideas,
and taking deeper draughts of the spirit of
that noble Craft whose whole tendency is
the elevation of character, and the directing
of his thoughts to a higher plane of existence here and the enjoyment of eternal bliss
hereafter.

We are informed "that it is a custom of
the Jews on the Sabbath to pay for the
privilege of unrolling the Sacred Law," so,
too, we who would uphold the law of our
Noble Institution, must pay for the privilege,
not in base coin, but in labor and research,
studying its principles, searching out its
design, and imbibing all of its Symbolism;
and the payment thus made will purchase a
rich Jewel.

At this stage of our progress we may ask ourselves the question, is the study of Freemasonry worthy the attention of a serious mind? Does it furnish a field of investigation in which the powerful and philosophic intellect can find ample scope for its researches?

As an answer to this question we will state that scholars of unquestioned ability, strength of intellect, and of deep, scientific research, have turned their attention to the study of Freemasonry. These have bequeathed to us the result of their laborious study. Surely, unless they found in their researches a congenial field of study, unless they perceived the deep philosophy which underlies and pervades the whole system of Masonry, it could not attract their serious attention.

Freemasonry has its enemies, who in *their* superior wisdom decry a system of whose very principles they are ignorant. Their positive statements of infalibility of criticism is, no doubt, unctious to their self conceit, but to the sober judgment of the well-informed they exhibit nothing but the traits of an unsound mind. Can a skeptic attack a creed which he does not understand? If he does, it is only because he is well satisfied with his own wisdom and self-sufficiency. When we bring before our minds the men of brilliant intellects and scientific renown who have astonished the world by their wonderful discoveries, what do we find? Let us mention, for instance, the case of Gall and Spurzheim, quoted by Mackay, who first gave to the world their wonderful discoveries in reference to the organization and functions of the brain — discoveries which have since wrought a marked revolution in the sciences of anatomy, physiology, and ethics — the Edinburg reviewers attempted to demolish these philosophers and their new system, but succeeded only in exposing their ignorance of the science they were discussing. Time, which is continually evolving truth out of error, and out of every intellectual conflict, has long since shown that the German philosophers were right, and that their Scottish critics were wrong."

The Alchemists of former generations, too, were, we know, derided as impostors, and Alchemy as a system of folly which was

engaged in only by fools or madmen, or
knaves. The patient researches of modern
investigators have shown, beyond the possibility of a doubt, that alchemists were
really religious philosophers. They show
also that the search after the elixir of life,
and the transmutation of metals to gold,
attributed to them, is baseless. They were a
class of men, pursuing with intense ardor,
the depths of philosophy in pursuit of the
higher phases of truth. They, like the
Freemasons, concealed under profound symbols, intelligible only to themselves, the
search after Divine Truth and the doctrine
of immortal life. "Truth was the gold
they eliminated from all mundane things,
and the immortality of the soul was the
elixir of everlasting life which perpetually
renewed youth, and took away the power
of death."

We have a parallel of this in Freemasonry.
Those who are foremost in their abuse of it
know the least of its principles, teaching,
and inner spirit. They know nothing of its
deep philosophy, or of the pure spiritual life
which it inculcates.

Freemasonry presents itself in two aspects to us.

1st. As a secret society possessing a peculiar ritual.

2d. As a philosophic society; that is founded on a philosophy which it teaches to its disciples.

From what we have already said we are now prepared to see that we may treat these as the *ritualistic* and *philosophic* aspects of Freemasonry.

The ritualistic element of Freemasonry refers to the due performance of the rites and ceremonies of the Order. Like what we know exists in the Church there are rubrics which instruct as to the proper conduct of Divine Worship. They teach both people and priests where to kneel and where to stand, and what part each is to take respectively, or both unitedly.

Also these rubrics instruct as to the proper occasions in which certain ceremonies are to be used. But do not all these refer to the inner organization of the Institution? They certainly do; in as much as they refer to the

manner in which its services shall be conducted. These may be performed in a very
perfunctory manner by those engaged in the
services, but that would not for an instant
argue that there was no higher or purer spirit
contained in and pervading these outward
forms and ceremonies. Neither has the
language of the ritual, and the form of the
ceremonies of Freemasonry, any more to do
with its philosophic element, no more than
the *rubrics* of the Church has to do *with
the faith* of the Church.

The rubrics are, of course, important to
the proper ordering of the service, but they
may be changed even in their most material
points, yet this would not affect the essential
faith of the Church. Neither would the Institution of Freemasonry be affected by a
change of its ritual. We do not deny the
importance of the ritual; for of course, it is
necessary to the due observance of the rites
and ceremonies, and also that a general uniformity be preserved. This only affects the
Fraternity itself. We never ask, and never
can ask for it, because of its secret character,
the consideration of scholars.

With the philosophic element and design of Freemasonry it is different. It is a subject of much importance. It is a subject entitled to the consideration, respect, and veneration of scholars.

[A great many theories have been advanced, and much discussion engaged in, by Masonic writers, as to the real origin, and the time when, and the place where, Freemasonry originated. Some trace it to the ancient mysteries, some to King Solomon's Temple, some to the Roman Colleges of Artificers, also to the Crusades of the Holy Land, to the Gilds of the Middle Ages, to the Stone Masons of Strasburg and Cologne, to the revolutionary struggle in England during the Commonwealth, and also to the secret efforts that had been made by the adherents of the House of Stuart to recover the throne. But whatever theory is adopted as to the time and place of its origin, of one fact we are cognizant, that for generations past, and within the records of history, it has presented to the world an unchanged organization. If we accept the theory that assigns to it one of the most recent periods of its organization,

that of the order of Freemasons at the building of the Cathedral of Strasburg in the year
1275. Since then upwards of six hundred
years have passed, and what aspect has Freemasonry presented during this time? It has
continued as a Brotherhood controlled by its
secret laws and discipline, engaged in architectural labors, and combining the elements
of Operative art, and religious speculations.
We admit that a change took place, *in this
particular*, that when there no longer existed
the necessity of the Operative element, it
was laid aside, and the Speculative aspect
only retained. In this change, however, it
is to be noted that the technical language,
the rules and regulations, the working tools,
and the discipline of the Operative Art were
all retained, the Master Builder of Strasburg
Cathedral, Erwin of Steinbach, with his disciples and followers, were engaged, under the
influence of a profoundly religious sentiment,
in the erection of a material building to be
devoted to the worship of the Almighty.
The Freemasons are similarly employed.
Their *material* is changed. They are actu-
ated by the same religious sentiments. They

employ themselves in the erection of a *Spir-itual Temple*. Is this puerile? Surely the long continuance of a Brotherhood employed in the same pursuit, changing only from a material to a spiritual character, but retain-ing its identity of organization, does it not demand for itself some respect, at least for its antiquity?]

But further, this Fraternity of Freemasons is in possession of certain symbols, myths, and legends, and above all, the GOLDEN LEGEND, which distinguish it from all other associations. These are all directed to the high aim of the purification of the heart, the elevation of the mind, and the development of the great fact of the immortality of the soul, and the resurrection to the life eternal.

The question as to where and when these symbols, myths, and legends came into the possession of Freemasonry, is certainly worthy the investigation of scholars, inas-much as they are inseparably connected with the history and development of the human mind. Is it to be accepted that the Stone-masons and Building Corporations of the Middle Ages invented them? Assuredly

not, because they are found in organizations
that existed many centuries before they (the
Builders of the Middle Ages) had existence.
In the chapter treating of the Ancient
Mysteries we have shown that the doctrine
of immortal life had been taught by the
same Symbolic mode.   The legend itself was
similar to the Masonic, differing only in
some details.   For Hiram, there was Dionysus
and other personages; for the Acacia, there
was the Myrtle.   The same mourning, the
same loss and discovery, the same rejoicings,
the same ineffable light, the same sacred
teaching of the holy name of God, and
the   immortality   of   the   soul   and   the
Resurrection, were identically the same in
substance.   Now, an ancient orator, who had
passed through these ancient initiations,
declares that "those who have endured the
initiations into the Mysteries entertain better
hopes both of the end of life and of the
eternal future."   This is the teaching, the
whole scope and design of the Master's
degree.   This Symbolism is to be found in
the Mysteries of Ancient Greece, those of
the Island of Samothracia, and among the

Old Egyptians "thousands of years before the glorious light of Christianity dawned upon the world to give the seal of its Master and Founder to the Divine Truth of the Resurrection."

This, however, will not prove, nor is it advanced by us as a design to prove, the descent of the Fraternity of Freemasons as now organized, from the religious Mysteries of antiquity. But it is advanced with a design to prove, and it does prove, "that there was an identity of design in all these institutions." Tracing the origin and source, the object and design of the different symbols, myths, and legends, will surely afford ample material for the profound study of the Masonic student. Who invented them? How and why have they been preserved? are important and interesting subjects for investigation.

Referring to the records of the past, we discover in the Island of Samothracia, near Greece, and in Egypt, an ancient priesthood teaching an existence in a future state by the use of symbols and legends. After the lapse of thousands of years, the same sym-

bolic and legendary mode of instruction is
employed to teach the same things. A comparatively modern institution is made the
repository for the preservation of these Symbolic designs. Between the remote past and
the present, similar associations succeed each
other, and, though they spread over different
countries, yet they all employed the same
Symbolic instruction, using substantially the
same symbols and the same mythical history.

What department of human knowledge
may be employed in the investigation of the
above? Is there not abundant scope for the
investigation of the departments of moral
and intellectual philosophy, and of historical
research, both ethical and archæological?
Is the solution of these problems to be
stigmatized as puerile? How vain, then,
and absurd, and foolish, are the objections of
a few narrow minds who can see no good in
anything outside of the narrow range of
their own prejudice. How groundless, how
unwarrantable, are the objections urged
against Freemasonry when its design is
directly connected with the grand subject of
the Brotherhood of Man. Itself forms a part

of those great brotherhoods which have filled the world for many ages. In fact, "the mind is carried back to such a remote period that some philosophic historians are of opinion that they must have derived the knowledge of the doctrine they taught in their Mystic assemblies from direct revelation through an ancient priesthood that gives no other evidence of its former existence but the result it produced."

As man has a three-fold nature, body, soul, and spirit, he needs something more than the gratification of his animal appetite. The mind requires food as well as the body, and surely, nothing is so well calculated to supply nutriment, and to act as a stimulus to the mind as the investigation of those subjects which relate to the development and progress of intellectual attainments, and the growth and development of the religious sentiment in man.

We must remember, too, that man was not made for himself alone. The stoic of old lived *for* and *in* himself. He was eminently selfish, but the truths of true religion, and true philosophy, teach and proclaim the

Brotherhood of man. What is our object in studying ancient history and ancient philosophy? Why are the productions of the old Greek and Roman philosophers and poets studied? Is it not that we may know what these old speculators thought, and that we may make a comparison as to the development of the mind of man as it then existed and as it now exists. "The study of the growth of intellectual philosophy, and the investigation of the mental and moral powers come home to us all as subjects of common interest."

We conclude by stating that as Freemasonry is one of those associations which furnish the evidence and the example of the progress of man, in intellectual, moral, and religious development, it may be well claimed for it, that its design, its history, and its philosophy, so far from being puerile, are well entitled to the respect of the world, and are worth the careful research of the scholar."

If we investigate the history and the proper spirit of Freemasonry in its speculative character, we can not fail to be strongly impressed with the fact that there is a pecu-

liar connection between it and civilization.
It may be said that they are co-existent. In
fact Freemasonry has ever been the result
of civilization. In the most ancient times
the spirit of Masonry and the spirit of civilization have always gone together. We can
historically show that the progress of
Masonry and that of civilization have been
identical. Where there is no appearance of
civilization there has been no Freemasonry.
Civilization surrounds and nurtures it; and
it in return purifies and elevates civilization.

We may assert that Freemasonry does not
exist among barbarous nations. They are
incapable of apprehending the truths which
the system contains; certainly, they could
never introduce, nor maintain if introduced,
the abstract doctrines of Divine Truth.

We have said that Speculative Freemasonry owes its birth to civilization, and
that it is never found and can never exist
among barbarous or savage races. But
wherever it exists, it exerts a reactionary
influence on the social condition of the people. Though we have instances of nations
retrograding in civilization, yet on the whole,

civilization is progressive. From all we can
ascertain from history and archæology we
must infer that the civilization of the ancient
world was inferior to that of the modern
world. Generally speaking, too, every century shows an advancement in the social,
intellectual, and moral condition of mankind.
Now, in every country and in every age in
which speculative systems analogous to
Freemasonry existed, they certainly proved
the means of extending and elevating civilization, and exerted a powerful influence in
the progressive steps of civilization towards
perfection. How does history illuminate us
in this matter? It brings before us the condition of the ancient heathen world and its
impure religion. It shows us how the
votaries of paganism bowed, in their ignorance to many gods and worshipped at their
shrines; and how that the Mythological history and character of these gods must
have corrupted the moral purity of their
worshippers. It is in this state of things that
the light of SPECULATIVE Phylosophy shines
upon and illumines the gross darkness
around. The "Ancient Mysteries" was

exerting a powerful influence upon a large class of aspirants and disciples by giving the higher and truer interpretation of the religious myths. In the shrines of the temples of Greece, and Rome, and Egypt, in the sacred caves of India, and in the consecrated groves of Scandinavia, Gaul, and Britain, these ancient sages were secretly divesting the Pagan faith of its polytheism, and of its anthropomorphic (like a man) deities, and were establishing a pure monotheism in its place, and illustrating by a peculiar symbolism the great dogmas — since taught in Freemasonry — of the unity of God, and the immortality of the soul."

We bring this down to modern times, when the religion of mankind under the benign, elevating, and pure influences of Christianity, does not require the like purification, still Speculative Masonry exerts an influence of a social character, tending to the elevation and extension of civilization.

Through its workings the social feelings have been strengthened and extended, the charities of life have had a new impulse given them in a spirit of refinement, and,

assuredly, as we know from actual facts, even
in the battle fields of Europe and this country, the bitterness of strife and the blood-
guiltiness of war, have been mitigated and
softened, and sometimes wholly obliterated.

From the foregoing we are led to these
conclusions, that as Speculative Masonry
owes its existence to a condition of civilization, so it in turn, by a reactionary influence,
proves a strong factor in extending, refining,
and elevating that which gave it birth by
advancing its moral, intellectual, and religious character.

CHAPTER VIII.

Before we enter into the direct history of Freemasonry we make a few observations on the meaning, usage, and derivation of the word " Mason." In our present mode of writing the word *Freemason*, we join the two words. Formerly, it was not so. " Free," and " Mason," were separated and written thus, Free Mason, or they were connected by a hyphen as Free-Mason. It does not appear that the term Freemason was generally used before the year 1670. The Old Constitutions always used the word Mason. Yet we find the word Free-mason used as early as the year 1550 in a book. "As the Free-mason hew the hard stones . . . . . . even so God the heavenly Freemason buildeth a Christian Church."

Numerous writers derive the word from different sources which would be too perplexing to the reader to give. We pass by many fanciful derivations of the word to say

that the most probable source from which the
word is derived is the word which expresses
a worker in stone, and that word is *Maconner*,
to build, hence the word Mason.

We now refer to the word "Free," as connected with "Mason." The original usage
of the word was in reference to the freedom
of the individual from the Gild or company
of incorporated Masons. It was not permitted to the Operative Masons, who were
not made free of the Gild or company, to
work with those who were. We may add
that the word "free" was first used in the
tenth century when the traveling Freemasons
were incorporated by the pope.

In reference to the phrase "Free and Accepted," the following account of the origin
of the term is taken from the Old Lectures
formerly used in England:

"The Masons who were selected to build
the Temple of Solomon were declared FREE,
and were exempted, together with their descendants from imposts, duties, and taxes.
They had also the privilege to bear arms. At
the destruction of the Temple by Nebuchad-
nezzer, the posterity of these Masons were

carried into captivity with the Ancient Jews. But the good will of Cyrus gave them permission to erect a second Temple having set them at liberty for that purpose. It is from this Epoch that we bear the name of Free and Accepted Masons."

Respecting the word "Accepted," we have only to remark that it is a term which is used to denote "initiation," or "received into the society." As we now use the term "*accepted*" we mean to express a distinction between the purely operative and speculative branches of Masonry.

We shall attempt no elaborate treatment of the direct history of Freemasonry in this little book. We endeavor, however, to give it in such a condensed manner as to bring the salient points into prominence before the reader. In doing this we shall lay aside as much as possible all credulity and imagination and approach the subject with as much critical research as we have material at command.

We have already given a definition of the word "Freemason." But how are we to understand the word *Masonry?* At present we generally use it as synonymous with Freemasonry. Now, if we accept it as such, then it follows that we must treat it according to the present form and organization of the Institution. Masonry certainly existed long anterior to the beginning of the eighteenth century. But unquestionably it received a restoration with a change of organization at this period.

What antiquity, then, can we assign to the Institution of Freemasonry? What incontrovertible evidence can we adduce in support of its antiquity? Remember we are speaking of the organization of Freemasonry in its integrity as it now exists.

We know that Fraternities analogous to the organization of Freemasonry existed before the period known as the revival in the year 1717. These were the Masonic Gilds of Europe, the Corporations of Stone Masons in Germany, the Traveling Freemasons of the Middle Ages, and the Colleges of Roman Architects. We have authentic, historical proof to show that these were similar in form, and design to the Masonic system. We speak of it in the sense of an architectural brotherhood, distinguished by fraternal ties, possessing signs, pass words, etc., which have not been essentially changed; and possessing also symbols and legends. These, instead of being materially changed, have been but developed and extended whilst undergoing a change from its Operative to its Speculative character.

If Freemasonry owes its origin to the Building Corporations, where did they come from, and where did they get their peculiar organization? They, too, must have had an historical beginning, and a pattern from which they received their peculiar organization. Their predecessors certainly were the Roman Artificers, who spread over Europe, with the invading and conquering armies of Rome. These Colleges of Roman Artificers, in their turn, have been traced to Numa. He gave them their two-fold character of Operative and religious, and in these characteristics they had been copied by similar associations of the Middle Ages.

From our previous statements we can understand that we must view Freemasonry in a two-fold sense: First, as a Society of

Speculative Architects engaged in the construction of a spiritual edifice, and in this respect, it is unquestionably developed from the Operative Architects of the tenth and succeeding centuries. They, in turn, claim to be derived from the Traveling Masons of Como, whose arch types were the Roman Colleges of Builders.

Furthermore, we must view Freemasonry in the other sense in which it manifests itself, and that is, as the " *Symbolic expression of a religious idea.*" In this light we see in it the teaching of the eternal. This is couched in both Symbol and Allegory, and taught by a legend. Where did the legend come from? Was it invented at the revival in 1717? or did those Corporations above named possess a Legend? Did the Operative Masonry of the seventeenth century have one? There is evidence that they did. And there is also proof that the Compagnons of France had theirs. These are known, and found to be similar in character to the Masonic legend; and to be connected with Solomon's Temple.

Here we would ask, did the Builders of the Middle Ages invent their legend, or did they obtain it from a source anterior to themselves?

The allegory of the Third Degree, as we now have it, is designed to teach by a symbolic representation, the Resurrection of the body, and eternal life after death.

The question for us to consider here is, can a similar allegory be found elsewhere?

For an answer to this question we must go back to a prehistoric period — to that era which connects it with the ancient Pagan world, and with the old priests of these mysteries. In this retrogression of time we do not deal with the present Organization of Freemasonry, because it did not then exist, but of certain characteristics peculiar to them and to Freemasonry. These characteristics are the very essence of both the ancient and Modern Association. "The *form* is different, the *spirit* is the same." Hence the analogy between the ancient mysteries and Freemasonry? We have in them the *germ* of our Order. But "they are not its cradle."

Certainly as a secret association containing "the symbolic expression of a religious idea" it is similar to the old mysteries, for they, too, employed symbolic teaching in the illustration of religious ideas. From whatever source they derived their symbolism and allegory, the Masonic Institution derives it directly or indirectly from the same.

How, then, shall we dispose of its connection with the Temple of Solomon? Was this connection merely accidental, or did the founders simply make an arbitrary selection? We are of opinion that neither method was adopted. But let us first consider the Symbolism of the Temple which is, and always has been, the most esteemed and cherished by Freemasons. It is the spiritualizing of the temple that constitutes the most prominent feature of the Order. In fact, it pervades the whole system, and gives it its most religious character. If we omit all reference to its rituals, legends, and traditions, what would we have left? Certainly nothing of Freemasonry. Each Lodge is a symbol of it, and each Master of a Lodge is a representative of the Jewish King, whilst every Mason represents a workman employed in the erection of the edifice.

The word temple is derived from the Latin

word *templum*, and this word is derived from
a root, which means to " cut off." Hence it
signifies a space cut off for a sacred purpose,
and separated from the adjoining profane
ground. It properly denoted a sacred enclosure where the Augurs consulted and the
omens were observed. It appears that the
Aryan races who originally came from
the table lands of India and settled nearly
the whole of Europe, were given to the
custom of worshipping in the open air, so
that their idea of a temple was the canopy
of the sky, and, in contradistinction to this,
the Shemitic idea of a place of worship was
a house temple. In time, however, a tent
was erected within the sacred enclosure
where the signs were observed, or more
properly, where their *contemplations* were
carried on. This, among the Greeks and
Romans, gave rise to the permanent temple
like the Hebrews.

We know that masonry derives its temple
Symbolism from the Jewish type, and makes
the temple the Symbol of the Lodge. It
has, however, borrowed from the Roman
temple one of the most significant words in

its whole system. The Latin word *speculor* means to observe, to look around. So when the observer of the omens watched the flight of the birds for either good or bad omens, he was said *speculari*, to speculate. Then it came to signify an observation of sacred things, and thus Freemasons become possessed of the technical word "Speculative" Masonry, denoting its religious design, and distinguishing it from the "Operative" or practical Masonry.

In its general scope, temple worship among the ancients denoted the religious sentiment in man and his advancement towards spiritual worship. Hence all the great nations of antiquity, no matter how they may differ in their objects of warship, had all their temples and orders of priests.

There can not be the slightest doubt, without doing violence to the most established facts, but that King Solomon's Temple, in its whole construction, was designed with a view to Symbolism. Nor was it difficult for the Jewish and Tyrian builders to adapt its construction to a science of Symbolism.

It will not, of course, be denied, but that

the Masonic Fraternity abundantly uses
Symbolic language representing the spiritual
nature of man by the image of the Material
temple. The language of the great Apostle
is, "Know ye not that ye are the temple of
God. If a man defile the temple of God,
him shall God destroy, for the temple of
God is holy, which temple ye are." And
again, "Your body is the temple of the Holy
Ghost." In the same spirit the Master
Mason adopts Solomon's Temple as the
Symbol of human life. As we have already
stated, the whole object of Masonry is the
search after truth, "they are directed to
build up this temple as a fitting receptacle
for truth when found, a place where it may
dwell, just as the ancient Jews built up
their great temple as a dwelling place for
Him who is the author of all truth."

This temple, however, was no abiding
place. Notwithstanding its splendor and
magnificence, it was but of a temporary
nature. This was evidenced by its spolia-
tion and destruction by Nebuchadnezzar.
Thus it became a fitting emblem of human
life in search of the truth — that Divine

Truth which should be the objective end of the quest of every soul of man. Here below, in a measure, it eludes his grasp, for he is ever sinning and repenting, ever falling and rising, at one time, healthful and vigorous, at another, sick and faint.

In higher Masonry, however, the Symbolism of the Temple is further developed. The Temple of the Master Mason and its Symbolism is left behind. Another is brought forward built on the ruins of the first. This is known as the Second Temple— the temple of Zerubbabel, and is adopted as the most prominent Symbol. As the first temple was designed to symbolize the mortal life that now is, so the symbolism of the second temple is that of eternal life which is to be. In the first the search after the Divine Truth was instituted, but in the second is seen the lost truth recovered. Was it not in this spirit our Divine Master used the Symbolic expression, ("Destroy this temple and in three days will I raise it up.") This referred to the temple of his body

We have said that we may trace the Institution of Freemasonry through the Masonic

Gilds of Europe, the Corporations of Stone Masons of Germany, the Traveling Free Masons of the Middle Ages, and then through the Roman Colleges of Architects to the ancient mysteries, and to a still higher source than these.

It will then be appropriate to give, in connection with the history of Freemasonry a brief sketch delineating the main features of these associations.

We introduce them thus :

First. *The Roman Colleges of Artificers.*

We are indebted to German writers for the first announcement of the connection between Freemasonry and the Roman Colleges of Artificers.

One of these, Krause, advanced the theory, that " Freemasonry, as it now exists, is indebted for all its characteristics, religious, and social, political and professional, its interior organization, its modes of thought and action, and its very design and object to the College of Artificers of the Romans, passing with but little characteristic changes through the *Architectural Gilds* of the Middle Ages up to the English Organization in the year

1717, so that he claims an almost absolute
identity between the Roman Colleges of
Numa, seven hundred years before Christ,
and the lodges of the nineteenth century.
We need not, according to his views, go
any further back in history, nor look to any
other series of events, nor trouble ourselves
with any other influences for the origin and
character of Masonry."

Before we accept this theory it is needful,
so far as authentic documents enable us to
do so, to investigate the characteristics of
these Roman Colleges.

As to their antiquity historians are pretty
well satisfied that they were established in
the reign of Numa, the second King of
Rome, and were, therefore, almost identical
in point of time, with the founding of Rome
itself. But it is considered that though it
was Numa who gave them the two-fold
religious and practical character, yet similar
corporations had previously existed amongst
the Tuscan Artificers.

When Rome commenced to conquer the
neighboring towns and territories, and when
she established herself as a Kingdom, she

had various tribes within her borders. When
Numa ascended the throne, he found that
this caused discordant feelings, and produced
diversities of interests. To counteract this
and to create a feeling of common nationality
and common interest, he established one common religion into curias and tribes, each
curia and tribe being composed of some of
the various nationalities which composed the
population of Rome.

He also divided the artisans into gilds or
corporations styled *Collegia* or "Colleges."
Each College comprised the artisans of a
particular calling or profession, having its
own regulation. These, of course, grew
with the growth of the Kingdom. There
were but nine gilds at first established, and
these were, the College of Musicians, of
Goldsmiths, of Carpenters, of Dyers, of Shoe-
makers, of Tanners, of Smiths, of Potters,
and the ninth was made up of all the trades
not mentioned in this list. In the course of
time these were greatly increased, and at a
period of about eighty years they were, by a
decree of the Senate, sought to be abolished.
They were, however, again revived, and en-

larged, and continued their existence during the Empire. With the conquest of the Roman armies, they were introduced into the provinces, and they outlived the Roman sway itself.

These Colleges appeared in diversified forms; they had certain features of organization common to all, but became somewhat varied in character as they became disseminated throughout the Empire. They were known by the name of Collegium or Corpus. They had, especially in the provinces, an intimate connection with the history of the people. The following were some of their general characteristics :

(1) Collegium (companions). The term originally expressed the idea of several persons joined together for some common purpose, but subsequently came to mean a body of persons, and the bond uniting them.

(2) A lawfully constituted "College" was *legitianum*, and an unlawful one *illegitianum*. Some of the Corporations were established by special laws, and others, no doubt were formed by the voluntary association of

individuals under some general laws for which they had legal authority.

(3) The College was divided into bodies of ten of one hundred men each, and were presided over by a master and wardens.

(4) They had a treasurer, secretary and archivist.

(5) As a corporation they could hold property, and could sue and be sued.

(6) An oath was administered to each candidate on his admission to the "College," and dues and subscriptions were collected to meet the general expenses.

There was one indispensible regulation which was, that no College could consist of less than three members. Hence the expression in the Civil Law, three makes a College.

These Colleges (companions) called themselves Brothers. "For amongst them," says Coote, "the dear bond of relationship, which though artificial, was that close alliance which a common sentiment can make. The Civil Law recognized, ratified, and extended, for allowing the assumption of kinship it

imposed on the Sodales another duty in ad-
dition to those already taken, by compelling
any one of them to accept the guardianship
of a child of a deceased Colleague."

We have said that at one time they had
been suppressed and again revived. In the
time of Theodosius there were in almost
every city companies of plebians similar to
those which existed in Rome. Whether this
arose from a voluntary combination or that
they were *compelled* to adopt some trade, we
do not know. These companies were established from time to time, by order of the
Emperor, as the general good of the community appeared to require. The artificers
in the several cities, especially in the East,
were exempted by Constantine from personal
duties. Amongst them the Architects and
Colleges of Workmen are frequently mentioned. There is no special mention made of
the masons. It is highly improbable but that
companies of stone cutters existed. It is
also highly probable that the College of
Artificers included workmen of various
crafts. This would seem to be the case from
a letter of the younger Pliny, when Procon-

sul of Asia Minor, to the Emperor Trajan, in which he informs him of a most destructive fire at Nicomedia, and requests permission to establish a College for the reconstruction of the city.

It was a fundamental principle of these Corporations that they conferred an hereditary privilege or duty. The son succeeded to the father in his occupation. In some cases the Civil Law permitted the admission of strangers.

Among the trades pursued by these Operative Fraternities must be included architecture, sculpture, and painting. The qualifications required entailed a study of a very laborious nature, certainly beyond that of the ordinary artisan. "The Masonic square, the level, and the mallet," displayed upon the memorial of the Roman architect, show that the mechanical art was considered important.

We may here remark that it is generally held "that from Constantinople, as the center of mechanical skill, radiated to distant countries a knowledge of art. According to Müller, corporations of builders of Grecian

birth were permitted outside the limits of
Byzantine Empire, to live and exercise a
judicial government among themselves according to the laws of the country to which
they owed allegiance. This principle or
doctrine of personal right to declare under
what law a citizen would elect to live, was
publicly recognized in all the legal codes of
Europe from the fall of Rome to the Thirteenth Century. This was denominated *his
profession of law.* Therefore, the Corporation of Artists, in retaining their connection
with Byzanthium, no doubt carried with
them such privilege of Grecian citizenship,
and when in Italy and other foreign countries, lived and governed themselves with
the well-known, established principles of
Roman law, one of which privileges was,
that at the time such association of builders
were introduced into Southern Europe during the reign of Theodosius, the undoubted
right of corporate recognition was given
them. Consequently, whenever their labor
was demanded throughout Europe, they were
recognized as a distinct and privileged class
of workmen, who, differing from the less

skilled artists of other countries, necessarily
formed a separate society, apart from that in
which they temporarily resided."

Steigleitz thinks, at least he records the
tradition, that when the Lombards, in the
Sixth and Seventh Centuries, were in possession of Northern Italy, the builders of Constantinople formed themselves into Guilds
and Associations, and that, on account of
having received from the Pope the privilege
of living according to their own laws and
ordinances, they were called Freemasons.

Another writer says: "It may be safely
asserted, that the junction of Byzantine
Corporations with Teutonic Gilds affords
the substantial basis of subsequent Lodge
appointments and ritualism, such as have
descended to modern Freemasonry."

We now revert to the points of resemblance between these Corporations and that
of the Masonic Institutions.   We have said
that it was a fundamental law of the Colleges
that there should be at least three to constitute a "College."   All Masons know that
this is a law of the Order.   They had also
their officers who most singularly corre-

sponded to the officers of a Masonic Lodge.
They were governed by a Magister, which is
identical in meaning to our word "Master."
These Colleges were partly religious, and had
a peculiar religious worship, hence each of
them had a *Sacerdos* (priest) who conducted
these religious ceremonies, corresponding to
the office of "Chaplain" in the Masonic
Lodge.

They had, also, their Master Masons, Fel-
low-crafts, and Apprentices.   Their place of
meeting was usually near a temple, and the
god to whom such temple was dedicated was
peculiarly worshipped by the members of the
adjacent College.   When Christianity dis-
placed the Pagan gods, some saint was
named as the patron of the *Gilds*, which, in
the Middle Ages, took the place of the
Roman Colleges.   From this the Freemasons
dedicate their lodges to the Saints John,
following the custom of the Corporation of
Builders.

Candidates for admission were elected in
the same manner as Freemasons are; that is,
by the consent of the members.   A Latin
word was used signifying "to be initiated

into the College." This word was more generally understood as "admitted or accepted
in a Fraternity," and so "made free of all the
privileges of the Gild or Corporation. This
is the same idea as that conveyed among the
Masons by the appellation "Free and Accepted."

Krause is authority for saying that they
cultivated the science of Symbolism in the
Symbolic use they made of the implements
of their Craft. If this is so, then it is in this
particular more than any other that there is
such a striking analogy between them and
the Masonic Fraternity of the present day.

The question presented to us for solution,
then, is, did Freemasonry, in the establishment of its Lodges, designedly adopt the
organization of these Corporations? Did
it take them as its model on which to
construct its system? Are Freemasons to
look to them and to the kindred Associations
which succeeded them as the source from
which was derived the *form* and *substance* of
their system?

As we have already stated, with the development of the growth and power of the

Republic, these Colleges extended to, and embraced, nearly every trade and profession. It is, however, only with the " Colleges of Architects " we have to concern ourselves, as the history of these alone are relevant to our investigation.

We know that the Romans were colonizers. They first either wholly or partially conquered a country, and then in the wake of their victorious legions they sent forth the colonists, who gradually civilized the barbarians and rude peoples among whom they dwelt.

To each legion a College of Artificers was attached, who accompanied it in all its campaigns; then, when the army colonized, they remained in the colony to introduce the seeds of Roman civilization.

When the Romans conquered England, they carried with them their Colleges of Architects. One of these, which accompanied Julius Cæsar, traveled into the northern part of the island, and established a colony there, which they called Eboracum (modern York). We know how celebrated that city is in the history of Masonry.

We know it is stated by some writers that the Romans left very little vestiges of their occupation of the island. For instance, one writer, Dr. Lingard, says: "By the conquest of the Saxons, the island was plunged into that state of barbarism from which it had been extricated by the Romans;" and again, Hallam, the historian, says: "No one traveling through England would discover that any people had ever inhabited it before the Saxons, save so far as mighty Rome left traces of her empire in some enduring walls."

These statements are contradicted by others, who take the position that the "Roman Britains suvirved all the barbarian conquests of the Saxons and Northmen, as well as the Picts and Scots; and that they retained their own laws, with its police and procedure, also their own lands with the tenure and proceedings appertaining to them;" and, further, all Roman cities were the foster mothers of those especially Roman Institutions — Colleges. The Anglo-Saxons found these institutions in full play when they came over here, and, with the cities in which they flourished, they left them to the

Romans, to make such use of them as they pleased, possibly ignoring them, certainly not interfering in their practice nor controlling their principles."

There are certainly abundant inscriptions and architectural remains existing, to show the enduring nature of the work executed by these Romans in Britain.

The religion of the Britons prior to the invasion of the Romans was Druidism. Paganism was the religion of the invaders. These, however, easily . harmonized. Long before this, however, Christianity had dawned upon the island. Quoting the language of Tertullian: "Britain, inaccessible to the Romans, was subdued by Christ." As a result of this conquest, the Colleges soon changed their character. They were transformed from the Pagan cultus to the doctrine and life of Christianity.

It is apparent, that we quote facts of history, when we say that when the Roman legions had been recalled from the provinces to repel the invasions of the northern barbarians, Britain was abandoned, and the inhabitants, including the Roman colonists were left to defend themselves as best they may. These, deprived of the protection of the Roman army, became an easy prey to their barbarian neighbors, the Picts and Scots, and to the Saxon invaders, and were compelled to seek refuge in Wales, the Isle of Man, and Ireland. The Roman Architects, converted to Christianity, accompanied them. In doing so, they severed all connection with the original Institution, and became simple Corporations of Builders.

Wherever they went, they introduced the art of building; and as the Christian faith spread and gained pre-eminence, churches, colleges, and cathedrals were built. Monasteries, too, were founded, and gradually there was much improvement in ecclesiastical architecture. This improvement, of course, extended to the civil or secular structures.

In the course of time, all the architectural skill of northern Europe and all the religious knowledge were confined to Ireland and parts of Scotland, from whence missionaries went to England, the Continent of Europe, even to the northern parts of Italy itself, carrying the blessings and enlightenment of Christianity with them.

We will not dwell longer on the history of this period further than to remark that the term "Scotland" was at one time applied exclusively to Ireland; and at another was applied indifferently to each, and sometimes included both. From this confusion has arisen the mistaken notion, that Scotland, as we now understand the country, as the northern portion of the Island of Great Britain, was the cradle from whence emanated the Christianity, ecclesiastical architecture, and OPERATIVE MASONRY, of the northern countries of Europe.

This historical error has been perpetuated in the language and traditions of Freemasonry up to the present day; as we may observe in the claim made for Kilwinning Abbey and the mountain of Heroden, where the first Lodge in Europe, it is claimed, was held.

After the advent of Augustine and his monks into Britain, and the long contests of the early British Church and the Papal power, which finally led to the submission of the British bishops to the power of the Pope; when the authority of the Pope was well established in Europe, and when, through ecclesiastical and civil exactions, combined at times with the genuine piety of the donors, giant cathedrals in all their magnificence began to be erected, then the Hierarchy of the Romish Church secured the services and skill of the Building Corpoi ations. These were taken under the protection of the Pope, and the prince bishops and other dignitaries of the Church, employed these "Traveling Freemasons," to build ecclesiastical and other structures.

From this time we find them scattered through almost every country in Europe, but still retaining their original characteristics. Their design was the same as the original "College"—they continued to be controlled by the same principles — and they retained all the distinctive features of a Gild or Corporation. Thus we see them retaining their identity with the Old Roman Colleges of Artificers.

In the year 926, in the City of York, in the north of England, an assembly of the

Craft was called for the purpose of framing a Constitution. Some, however, deny that such a meeting ever took place. Until comparatively recent times, however, it was accepted by the Craft as authentic history. In view of its denial by adversaries, and of its acceptance by friends, what course are we to pursue to arrive at the truth? We first place before us what is considered legendary or traditional, and then what we can obtain of authentic history, founded on the researches of the latest investigations.

Of all the old Constitutions extant, the most ancient is what is known as the Halliwell Manuscript, the date of which is the year 1390. A version of the legend is contained in this manuscript. As it may be interesting to some of the readers of this book to know the words of the original of this passage, and as all may not be able to understand the Old English in which it is written, we give what may be called a translation of the version in Modern English. This I copy from Mackey's "Encyclopedia of Freemasonry."

"This Craft came into England, as I tell

you, in the time of good King Athelstane's reign; he made then both hall, and also bower and lofty temples of great honor, to take his recreation in both day and night, and to worship his God with all his might. This good lord loved this Craft full well, and purposed to strengthen it in every part on account of various defects that he discovered in the Craft. He sent about in all the land after all the Masons of the Craft, to come straight to him, to amend all these defects by good counsel, if it might so happen. He then permitted an assembly to be made of divers lords in their rank, dukes, earls, and barons, also knights, squires, and many more, and the great burgesses of that city, they were all there in their degree, these were there, each one in every way to make laws for the estate of these Masons. There they sought by their wisdom how they might govern it; there they found out fifteen articles, and there they made fifteen points."

The next document in which it is given is in what is known as the "Cooke Manuscript," date 1490. This contains a fuller statement than the above.

Again in the "Landsdowne Manuscript," which bears the date of 1560, the account is still further developed, and in it the name of Prince Edwin first appears.

All the later manuscripts contain it. They all resemble this one (Landsdowne's), and they all appear to be copies of some original manuscript.

A "Book of Constitutions" was published by Dr. Anderson in the year 1723. In this he claims "to have collected the history of Freemasonry from their general records, and their faithful traditions of many ages." He records the account taken, as he expresses it, from "a certain record of Freemasonry written in the reign of King Edward IV. Preston, the Masonic historian, says "that this manuscript is said to have been in the possession of the famous Elias Ashmole."

Anderson published a second edition of the "Constitutions" in the year 1738, and gives in it the account of the York Assembly, the substance of which is as follows:

"That though the ancient records of the Brotherhood had been lost in England during the wars with the Danes, yet King

Athelstane, the grandson of Alfred the
Great (he who had translated the Holy Bible
into the Saxon language), when he had
restored rest and peace unto the land, built
many great works, and encouraged many
Masons from France and elsewhere to come
to England. These brought with them the
Charges and Regulations of the foreign
Lodges, and prevailed with the King to
increase the wages.

"Prince Edwin, the King's brother, being
taught Geometrie and Masonry, from love to
the Craft because of its honorable principles,
purchased from the King a Charter to enable
the Free Masons to govern themselves.

"Then Prince Edwin summoned all the
Free and Accepted Masons in the realm to
meet him in the Congregation at York, who
came and formed the Grand Lodge under
him as their Grand Master, A. D. 926.

"They brought with them many old writings and records of the Craft, and from these
records framed the Constitutions of the
English Lodges, and made a Law for themselves to preserve and observe the same in
all time coming," etc.

This is commonly known as the "York legend," and it is contained, as we have seen, in all the old manuscripts since the year 1390.

Is there a reasonable probability that such an assembly of Operative Masons met at York about the date mentioned, 926? Certainly, it is just what we may expect from the general character of King Athelstane. "He was a patron of learning, he built monasteries and churches, encouraged the translation of the Scriptures, and gave charters to many Operative companies, and free Gilds were established in his reign." If this were his character, what is there improbable that he should have given his protection and encouragement to the Operative Masons?

We may then draw the following conclusion from what has been said in reference to this Assembly: It is most likely the original document above referred to has been lost, that it is very evident from the contents of the different manuscripts that they had a common source, and that that common source was the original Constitution adopted at the Assembly held at York in the year

A. D. 926. This, of course, has been doubted and denied; so have various other facts of history.

We may here mention that a similar Assembly was held at Strasburg, in Germany, in the year 1275, when Edwin of Steinbach took charge of the works at Strasburg Cathedral; and when he had summoned Masons from Germany, Italy, and England, he formed with them a Brotherhood from which a Freemasonry, based on the English system, was established. Strasburg takes the place in German Masonry similar to York in English Masonry. This has been so engrafted in the minds of the German Fraternity, that even now the stone masons of Saxony still look upon the Strasburg Lodge as their chief Lodge.

CHAPTER IX.

The history of the "Traveling Freemasons" is very interesting to every Masonic student. They appear in that portion of the history of Europe designated the Middle Ages, beginning about the tenth century. At this time the whole of Christian Europe was employed in the erection of religious houses and places of worship, as well as in building castles, fortresses, etc. At this time an association of workmen passed from country to country, and from one city or province to another. These were the "Traveling Freemasons." There is hardly any country in Europe in which there are not found structures in greater or less state of preservation, attesting the skill of these, our **Masonic** ancestors.

Several writers treat of them. Goodwin, in the "*Builder*" says: "There are few points in the Middle Ages more pleasing to look back upon than the existence of the associated Masons; they are the bright spot in the general darkness of that period, the patch of verdure when all around is darkness."

Another writer says, that these Colleges of Artisans, which were instituted at Rome by Numa in the year 714, B. C., and whose members were originally Greeks, imported by this lawgiver for the purpose of embellishing the city over which he reigned. They continued to exist as well-established corporations throughout all the succeeding years of the Kingdom, the republic, and the empire.

As we may well suppose, these Fraternities suffered during the barbarian invasions. But when Europe became Christian, they flourished. The dignitaries of the Church became their patrons and friends. In the tenth century they were established as corporations or gilds in Lombardy. After the fall and declension of Rome, owing to a combination of circumstances, Lombardy became the great centre of trade, refinement, art, and literature. In consequence of this and of its great commercial life the first *gilds* were established.

Of the many trades engaged in by these Lombards the art of building held a high rank. The city of Como, situated here in Lombardy, became famous for its architects, so much so, that they were everywhere known as "Masters from Como."

Mr. Hope (quoted by Mackey), in "*Historical Essay on Architecture,*" gives the following able and interesting description of them:

"We can not, then, wonder that, at a period when artificers and artists of every class, from those of the most mechanical to those of the most intellectual nature, formed themselves into exclusive corporations, Architects — whose art may be said to offer the most exact medium between those of the most urgent necessity and those of mere ornament, or, indeed, in its wide span, to embrace both — should, above all others, have associated themselves into similar bodies, which, in conformity to the general style of such Corporations, assumed that of Free and Accepted Masons, and was composed of those members who, after a regular passage through the different fixed stages of

Apprenticeship, were received as Masters, and entitled to exercise the profession on their own account.

"In an age, however, in which lay individuals, from the lowest subject to the soveign himself, seldom built, except for mere shelter and safety — seldom sought, nay, rather avoided, in their dwellings an elegance which might lessen their security; in which even the community, collectively, in its public and general capacity, divided into component parts less numerous and less varied, required not those numerous public edifices which we possess, either for business or for pleasure; thus, when neither domestic nor civic architecture of any sort demanded great ability or afforded great employment, churches and monasteries were the only buildings required to combine extent and elegance, and sacred architecture alone could furnish an extensive field for the exercise of great skill. Lombardy itself, opulent and thriving as it was, compared to other countries, soon became nearly saturated with the necessary edifices, and unable to give these companies of Free and Accepted Masons a

longer continuance of sufficient custom, or
to render the further maintenance of their
exclusive privileges of great benefit to man
at home. But if to the south of the Alps an
earlier civilization had at last caused the
number of architects to exceed that of new
buildings wanted, it fared otherwise in the
north of Europe, where a gradually spread-
ing Christianity began on every side to pro-
duce a want of sacred edifices, of churches
and monasteries, to design which architects
dwelt not on the spot.

"Those Italian Corporations of Builders,
therefore, whose services ceased to be necessary in the countries where they had arisen,
now began to look abroad to those northern
climes for the employment which they no
longer found at home, and a certain number
formed and united themselves into a single
greater association or fraternity, which proposed to seek for occupation beyond its
native land, and in any ruder foreign region,
however remote, where new religious edifices, and skillful artists to erect them, were
wanted, to offer their services and bend their
steps to undertake the work."

Now commenced their period of special prosperity. They passed from Lombardy and spread themselves all over Europe wherever there was a demand for their services. Special favors were conferred on them. They were encouraged on all sides, by the Popes especially, who granted them privileges wherever they went. "They obtained a monopoly for the erection of all sacred buildings. They were even declared independent of the sovereign in whose territory they had been temporarily residing, and subject only to their own laws." They could fix their wages, they paid no taxes, and none, excepting a member of the Fraternity, could oppose or compete with them. In reference to these Artificers one of the Popes says: "These regulations have been made after the example of Hiram, King of Tyre, when he sent artisans to King Solomon for the purpose of building the Temple of Jerusalem."

From Europe they passed to England and Scotland, and have left an enduring memorial of their residence there, whilst erecting an abbey in the parish of Kilwinning, by plant-

ing the germ of Scottish Freemasonry, which
has been perpetuated through the Grand
Lodge of Scotland to the present time.

At this time the element of the non-
working members began to be united with
the Craft. We summarize Mr. Hope's account of it, given by Mackey: "They were
often obliged from the most distant regions
to seek common places of rendezvous and
departure to places of employment equally
distant, and that at an era when travelers
met on the road every species of obstruction,
when no inns existed at which to purchase
hospitality, but lords dwelt everywhere.
These prevented their tenants from way-
laying the traveler, because, like the killing
of game, they considered it their own peculiar privilege. They frequently, for greater
security of travel, engaged themselves with
parties not professionally connected with
them. They established institutions for
their needy brothers, but lest those who did
not belong to their brotherhood should avail
themselves surreptitiously of their advantages, they framed signs of mutual recognition such as carefully concealed from the

uninitiated the knowledge of their mysteries.
Thus provided for, they were able to obey
any summons issued to them to proceed to
any distant place with the least possible
delay. The missionaries of the Church of
Rome diffused themselves all over Europe to
instruct the nations and to establish their
allegiance to the Pope, took care not only to
make them feel the want of churches and
monasteries, but also to learn the manner in
which the wants may be supplied. Indeed,
they themselves, usually undertook the supply, and it may be asserted that a new
Apostle of the Gospel no sooner arrived in
the remotest corner of Europe, either to
convert the inhabitants to Christianity or to
introduce among them a new religious order,
than speedily followed a tribe of itinerant
Free Masons to back him, and to provide
the inhabitants with the necessary places of
worship and reception.

" Thus ushered in, by their interior
arrangements, assured of assistance and of
safety on the road, and by the bulls of the
Pope and the support of his ministers
abroad, of every species of immunity and

preference at their place of destination,
bodies of Freemasons dispersed themselves
in every direction; every day began to advance further, and proceed from country to
country, to the utmost verge of the faithful,
in order to answer the increasing demand
for them, or to seek more distant custom.

Wherever these Fraternities were worked,
or were located, they were governed according to uniform rules. They erected Lodges
in the vicinity of their work, and over every
ten men was placed a warden. He paid them
their wages, and saw that there was no waste
nor loss of tools. A master (magister) was
placed over all, who superintended the whole
work. There is an ancient document or
register which contains the regulations of
the Masons at Strasburg, who built that
noble structure — its Cathedral. We have
elsewhere stated that it was commenced in
the year 1277, under the superintendence of
Edwin of Steinbach. " This is considered
the noblest specimen of the Gothic style of
Architecture." The Masons employed in its
construction were divided into Apprentices,
Fellows, and Masters. Where they resided

in companies was called a Lodge. They
used the implements of Masonry as emblems
and wore them as insignia. They had signs
and pass-words as modes of recognition.
They used peculiar rites and ceremonies in
the initiation of members. Ecclesiastics and
many others of distinction, who were not
Operative Masons, were admitted to their
Fraternity.

These Masons of Strasburg became famous
throughout Germany. The Masters of Lodges
in several of the States of Germany met at
Ratisbon in the year 1459 and adopted an
act of union declaring the Master of the
Strasburg Cathedral perpetual Grand Master
of the Fraternity of Freemasons of Germany.

These "Traveling Freemasons" entered
Switzerland, France, also England and Scotland. At a period not long subsequent to
their departure from Lombardy, Corporations or Gilds of Operative Architects or
Masons existed in England.

Many of the old Charges for the better
government of the Craft are preserved and
found in our Books of Constitutions, demon-

strating the fact that they were intended for the government and guidance of a strictly Operative Association.

In the summary of the history of these most interesting and singular Associations, and viewing their Constitutions, we are constrained to hold that they were strictly religious, although, originally, all Operatives. Like their ancestors who were employed in the building of the magnificent Temple of Jerusalem, they devoted themselves to labor for the " House of the Lord." So that all along in the history of the Institution of Freemasonry it has ever exhibited the traits of a religious Fraternity.

The Operatives or artisans of the times we are speaking of were not educated men. They had *skill* to execute, but they had not the *brain* to invent and to embellish. They were of necessity compelled to seek the assistance of, principally, the ecclesiastics, who pretty well monopolized the learning of the time. On making this statement we do not intend to convey the idea that there were not among these Operatives, or rather Architects, those who were pre-eminently qualified to plan and to execute what their brain conceived. Otherwise the marvelous structures of beauty and symmetry could never have been erected. But we speak generally. The princes, nobles, and prelates who were admitted among them constituted the *germ* of the Speculative element which gradually formed its predominating, and now wholly, its distinctive character.

The Gilds, which by some writers are claimed to be of English origin, the Stonemasons of Germany, the Compagnons de la Tour of France are but certain modifications, although possessing some distinguishing characteristics, of the Associations of the "Roman Colleges of Architects," and of the "Traveling Masons." We will not, therefore, treat separately of them.

But we have not yet exhausted all the possible sources from which Freemasonry is said to be derived. We shall continue the subject in the next chapter.

CHAPTER X.

There are those who implicitly believe that the Fraternity of Freemasonry had its origin and flourished in Judea in the reign of King Solomon, and that from that time it has descended, in all its integrity, to our day, and that the Freemasonry of that time is identical in all its essential points with our modern Institution. Those who deny this theory say, if that is so, then the chain of descent can be traced in unbroken succession from then until now. There must have existed in Palestine a society or association which preserved the landmarks of the Order. The reply is: Yes, we can point to such — *the Essenes*. When we come to trace their history we find a remarkable coincidence in the nature, objects, and ceremonies of the two Institutions.

Jewish philosophers, heathen writers, and Christian historians mention this peculiar and interesting people.

(236)

We know from sacred history that when our Lord Jesus Christ made his appearance in Judea, there then existed there three prominent religious sects; namely, the Pharisees, the Sadducees, and the Essenes.

The precise period in which this last named Order of Judaism first developed itself is not definitely known. Three writers mention certain facts in connection with its appearance. These are Philo, Josephus, and Pliny.

Philo says it was instituted by Moses.

Pliny says: "Towards the West (of the Dead Sea) are the Essenes. They are a heretical society, marvelous beyond all others throughout the whole earth. They live without any women, without money, and in the company of palm trees. Their ranks are daily made up of the company of the multitudes who resort to them, and who being weary of life. Thus it is that through thousands of ages, incredible to relate, this people prolongs its existence without any one being born among them, so fruitful to them are the weary lives of others."

Josephus, speaking in general terms of

them, says that they existed ever since the time of the fathers.

All these statements show that secret societies existed from a very remote period of antiquity. We shall show that this was a secret society.

It is thought by some writers that they were not a distinct Jewish sect, that they never completely severed themselves from the rest of the community; that they were simply an order of Judaism; in fact, that they held ultra-pharasaical doctrines and usages; that they were the same as the Chasidim. If this is so, then here is one feature in which they closely resemble Freemasonry. There is, however, a fundamental distinction between them. Freemasonry adopts a spirit of universal tolerance to all religions, whilst it is itself Christian; but the Essenes were wholly Jewish in doctrine, usage, and scope, and confined its membership exclusively to Jews.

The Jewish historian, Josephus, speaks definitely of them as existing in the days of the Maccabeas. It is thought that our Savior whilst on earth was a member of this Fraternity. The idea, however, is but purely inferential.

We have mention of them as far down as 400 A. D. Epiphanius, Bishop of Constantia and Metropolitan of Cyprus, who was born in Palestine early in the Fourth Century, and died in the year 402 A. D., alludes several times to them in his celebrated work, " Against the Heretics."

At the establishment of Christianity they appear to be amongst the earliest who embraced its faith.

The Essenes were very strict in their observance of the Mosaic law of purity. They regarded the written law of God with the utmost veneration. Their highest aim in life was to become the Temples of the Holy Ghost, when they could prophesy, perform miracles, effect cures, and, like Elias, be the forerunners of the Messiah. This was regarded as the last stage of perfection, which could only be reached by gradual growth in holiness through strict observance of the Law. They abstained from using oaths, because they regarded the invo-

cation in swearing of anything which represents God's glory a desecration.

According to tradition there were four
degrees of purity:

First — The ordinary purity required of
every worshipper in the Temple.

Second — The higher degree of purity
required of every one who would eat the
leaven offering.

Third — The still higher degree of purity
required of those who partake of the sacrifices.

Fourth — The degree of purity required
of those who sprinkle the water absolving
from sin.

The first of these was obligatory, the
others voluntary.

They had a community of goods, and the
wants of all supplied from a common treas-
ury. Consequently there was no distinction
of rich and poor among them. The only
difference of rank among them was the
degree of the Order they attained, and
that was wholly dependent on the degree
of holiness attained. They lived peace-
ably with all men. Slavery and war

were abomination to them. They were governed by a president, who was elected by the whole community. A member, for violation of rules and other offenses might, after due trial, be excommunicated or expelled.

They held no communication with those outside their own community, and were therefore compelled to raise their own supplies. They rose before sunrise, and never talked of wordly matters before they had assembled and prayed together. Some occupied themselves in healing the sick, some in instructing the young; but all of them devoted certain hours to studying the Mysteries of nature and of Revelation, and of Astronomy.

They rigorously observed the Sabbath. Ten persons constituted a legal number to hold Divine Service. They had no ordained minister, and the distinctive orders of the Brotherhood, as well as the Mysteries connected with the Tetragrammaton and the angelic worlds, were the prominent topics of the Sabbath day's instruction.

They studied the Scriptures, and contemplated especially on the *expository name* of

God. They were a holy Brotherhood, and
engaged in the labors of works of mercy
and charity. They curbed their anger and
passions. They were faithful. No traducers
or maligners of character. They were ministers of peace.

The novice before admission to the Fraternity received a copy of the regulations of
the Order, and was presented with a *spade*,
an *apron*, and a *white robe*. When the candidate reached the highest degree, called the
disciple or companion, he was bound by a
solemn obligation to love God, to be just
to all men, to practice charity, to maintain
truth, and to conceal the secrets of the Society and the Mysteries of the Tetragrammaton, and the other names of God.

They were truly a remarkable people.
Probably the world never produced a people more earnest or more desirous in their
intense earnestness to serve God, and to
reach that purity and holiness after which
they aspired. "Their absolute confidence in
God and resignation to the will of Providence, their uniformly holy and unselfish
life, their unbounded virtue and utter con-

tempt for worldly fame and riches; their
industry, temperance, modesty and simplicity of life; their contentment of life
and cheerfulness of disposition, their love
of order and abhorrence of even the sem-
blance of falsehood, their benevolence and
philanthropy, their love for the brethren and
their following peace with all men, their ten-
der regard for children and reverence and
anxious care for the aged, their attendance
on the sick and readiness to relieve the
distressed, their humility and magnanimity,
their firmness of character and power to
subdue their passions, their heroic endur-
ance under the most agonizing sufferings
for righteousness sake, and their cheerfully
looking forward to death, as releasing their
immortal souls from the bonds of the body
to be forever in a state of bliss with their
Creator — have hardly found a parallel in
the history of mankind."

Like Freemasons, they instructed their
newly-made members in the principles and
knowledge of the Order. No women were
admitted among them. They had particular
signs for recognizing each other, which bear

a striking resemblance to those of Freemasonry. They had colleges or places of retire-
ment, where they contemplated and managed
the affairs of the Society. Treasurers were
appointed in every town to relieve the wants
of strangers.

Lawrie, in his *History of Freemasonry*, is
of the opinion that the similarity between
the Masonic and Essenian systems is owing
to the fact that they must have a common
origin. He classes them with the "Chasidim," an "Association of Architects who
were connected with the building of Solomon's Temple." The Chasidim certainly
existed, but we do not know that they were
a Society of Architects. It is thought they
were a Jewish sect who held the Temple
in especial honor. Certainly there was a
similar spirit of Brotherhood, but then was
not this the "inherent principle which prevailed in all ages of the civilized world —
the inherent principles of which, as the
results of any Fraternity — all the members
of which are engaged in the same pursuit
and assenting to the same religious creed —

are brotherly ₁ove, charity, and that secrecy which gives them their exclusiveness."

In tracing the history of Corporations or Fraternities bearing in their principles or organization a resemblance to the Masonic Fraternity we can not omit a reference to those called *"Culdees."* Much controversy exists among writers as to *whom* the word should be applied. Should it be used only in reference to the disciples of St. Columba?

It is an historical fact that when Augustine, the monk, with his associates, came to England in the commencement of the Sixth Century, for the purpose of converting the natives to Christianity, that he found already a British Church existing there having their own priests and followers. These were distinguished both for their purity of doctrine and life. These were called " *Culdees*," a name which, according to some, means " *Cultores Die*," or worshippers of God. According to others it means, derived from the Gaelic language, *Cuildich*, a secluded corner, alluding to their hermit or retired mode of life. They are said to have come with the Roman legions to Britain, and that

they were in some way connected with the
Roman Colleges. If this is so, then they
must be considered only as a society composed of certain individuals who were members of the British Church.

The chief seat of the Culdees was in the
island of Iona, where St. Columba established his principal monastery. Columba
came to Iona, with twelve followers, in the
year 563. In the year 600 they established
other monasteries at Avernethy, Dienkeld,
St. Andrew's, Dumferline, Brechin, Melrose,
and other places in Scotland.

The question to consider is were the disciples of St. Columba and the Culdees identical? What relation, if any, existed between
them? It is thought that there is nothing
exclusive in the term, but that it represents
the clerics and monks of the ancient Celtic
Church, as well as those who were their successors.

Dr. Reeves denies that they were a peculiar
order or that they were a distinct body in the
Church, but that the word *Culdee* was a
distinctive term applied to them as denoting
their ascetism. It is true that after the lapse

of centuries they are found mentioned in connection with churches which St. Columba and his disciples had founded. It is only when the Columban monks had been expelled from what was known as the Kingdom of the Picts that we find the term used. The name is unknown in the works of Bede and other writers contemporary with or immediately succeeding him. In this connection we must remember that it is not because a *name* does not occur that a thing does not exist. It is not because the name *Culdee* is not found mentioned before the year 800 A. D. that *Culdees* did not exist. There was no special necessity for it. Whilst the Celtic monks alone existed in the country there was no need of a special name to distinguish them.

Whatever opinion may be held as to the derivation of the word and its use for the first time, it can, in its present form, be traced to the year 1526.

In the Seventh Century the terms of the Continental Anchorites begin to appear in an Irish form as applied to the Monkish

Orders. Irish Anchorites had the term *Ceile-De* applied to them.

It can not be said that Scotland was the original seat of the Culdees. Nor yet that it was their only seat. The Canons of the York Constitutions were called Culdees in the reign of King Athelstane, and certainly Ireland had numerous establishments of the Culdees, and had retained their name at Armagh to the time of Archbishop Usher in the Seventeenth Century. They also resided in Wales in an unmarried state, and leading holy lives. Their history is indeed but fragmentary. From extracts from ecclesiastical records between the Eighth and Sixteenth Centuries we have mention of them, and from the period of the Eighth Century, when they conformed to the Roman ritual. Then their individuality virtually ceased, and, in a sense, their usefulness, too.

The Irish did not consider them peculiar to their island. This appears from a life of St. Patrick in the early part of the Eighth Century, as also from some entries in the Annals of the *Four Masters*. Irish annals of unquestioned authority relate that in the

year 919 a Ceile-De came across the sea
westward to establish laws. This is supposed by Irish archæologists to bring the
Irish into conformity with the rule for
canons, which had been enacted in 816 at
the council of Aix-la-Chapelle.

The service book with musical notation,
from which the Culdees as the choir of St.
Patrick's Cathedral sang, is still preserved
in the library of Trinity College, Dublin.

The chief interest of Scottish Culdeeism
arises from the supposition that it had its
origin in Iona. Dr. Lanigan denies that the
name ever occurs in the annals of Iona.
After the year 1382 the name and office in
Scotland entirely disappears.

It is not historically certain at what date
the Christain faith was first introduced into
Britain. It is most probable that at first it
was brought from the East. To a certain
extent Druidism must have been affected by
the Paganism of the Empire at the time
when Christianity first appeared in Britain.
It is reasonable to suppose that the name
originated with the Clerics of the early
British Church, who were styled the " Cul-

tores Deorum " — the " worshippers of the
Gods " — gradually changing to the form
" Cultores Die," worshippers of the true
God.

Many believe that there was a connection
between the Culdees and the Roman Masonic
Colleges. It appears, however, that architecture was not their chief concern. " They
sought principally to socialize and civilize
mankind by imparting to them the knowledge of those pure principles which they
taught in their Lodges."

Others, however, " think that the Culdees
had organized within themselves and as a
part of their social system Corporations of
Builders, and that they exercised the architectural art in the construction of many
sacred edifices in Scotland, Ireland, and
Wales, and even in other countries of northern Europe."

It is also claimed, as we have said, that
the York Constitutions of the Tenth Century were derived from them.

Masonic writers also claim that between
these Apostolic Christians and the early
Masonry of Scotland and Ireland there was
a close connection.

CHAPTER XI.

We now place before our readers some of the beautiful symbols of Freemasonry.

What is a symbol? It is an outward sign to which a spiritual idea is attached.

The early Christians gave the name symbol to all their rites and ceremonies which had a religious significance. The early nations of the world, and especially the Egyptians, communicated the knowledge of their "Mysteries," or esoteric philosophy, by means of symbols. "The first learning of the world was by means of symbols." "The tree of life" in the garden of Eden, and the "flaming sword" guarding the way of the tree of life, were visible signs or symbols representative of other things. "The wisdom of the Chaldeans, Phœnicians, Egyptians, Jews, of Zoroaster, Pythagoras, Socrates, Plato, and of all the ancients that have come to our hand, is symbolic."

The word itself, "symbol," signifies a com-

parison of one thing with another.   Emblem
and symbol are often used interchangeably
as denoting the same 'thing in Masonry, and
embrace a moral conception.   For instance,
the *plumb* is a symbol of rectitude of character and conduct, the *level* is a symbol of
equality as denoting that all true and worthy
Masons are equal.   The outward qualities
and uses of these will always associate
themselves in our minds with the moral
qualities they are intended to represent.

Symbolism appeals powerfully to our mental conceptions.   How much more when, in
the infancy of the human race, language
conveyed but few ideas.   "Then visible symbols were the most vivid means of acting
upon the minds of ignorant hearers."   We
may in this manner see how natural it was
that the teachings of the first religions were
pre-eminently symbolic.

The letters of the alphabet are symbols of
certain sounds.   Language itself is the symbol of certain ideas.

Barlow, in his *Essays on Symbolism*, says:
" Symbolical representation of things sacred
were coeval with religion itself as a system

of doctrine appealing to sense, and have
accompanied its transmission to ourselves
from the earliest known period of monu-
mental history.

"Egyptian tombs and stiles exhibit religious symbols still in use among the Christians. Similar forms, with corresponding
meanings, though under different names, are
found among the Indians, and are seen on
the monuments of the Assyrians, the Etrus-
cans, and the Greeks.

"The Hebrews borrowed much of their
early religious symbolism from the Egyptians, the latter from the Babylonians, and
through them this symbolic imagery, both
verbal and objective, has descended to ourselves.

"The Egyptian priests were great pro-
ficients in Symbolism, and so were the
Chaldeans, and so were Moses and the
prophets, and the Jewish doctors generally—
and so were many of the early Fathers of
the Church, especially the Greek fathers.

"Philo, of Alexandria, was very learned
in Symbolism, and the Evangelist St. John
makes much use of it.

" The early Christian Architects, Sculptors and Painters drank deep of Symbolic lore and reproduced it in their works."

All the teaching of Freemasonry is given by means of Symbols. Being " founded as a Speculative Science on an Operative art, it takes the working tools of Masonry, the terms of architecture, the temple of Solomon, and everything that is connected with its traditional history, and adopting them as Symbols it teaches its great moral and philosophical lessons by this system of Symbolism. But its symbols are not confined to material objects as were the hieroglyphics of the Egyptians. Its myths and legends are also Symbolic for the most part. * * * These myths and legends when interpreted as a symbol impress the mind with some great spiritual and philosophic truth. The legends of Masonry are parables, and a parable is only a spoken symbol. By its utterance spiritual things are better understood, and make a deeper impression on the attentive mind."

The *All-Seeing-Eye*. This is a Symbol of God used by ancient nations, and transmitted to the Freemasons. It was used by both Hebrews and Egyptians who naturally selected it as being the organ of discernment, and watchfulness, and the eye of God, that which never slumbers nor sleeps, but indicates the watchfulness and care of God over the universe and all the works thereof. The use of this Symbol is in many passages used in the Old Testament Scriptures. The Psalmist says, "the eyes of the Lord are upon the righteous, and his eyes are open to their cry." Again, where it is said, "Behold He that keepeth Israel shall neither slumber nor sleep."

The ancient Egyptians represented their god Osiris by the Symbol of an open eye, and placed it as an hieroglyph ic in their temples.

The ALL-SEEING-EYE represents in Masonry the Omnipresence of God — his guardian and preserving character — as is alluded to by Solomon in the Book of Proverbs, "The eyes of Jehovah are in every place, beholding the evil and the good."

The *altar* is a very significant Symbolism in Freemasonry. It is a structure whereon

divine worship, such as sacrifices, oblations
and prayers were offered. We learn from
history that altars were erected and used
long before temples. When Noah left the
Ark, he built an altar unto the Lord.

It appears that both among the Gentiles
and Hebrews altars were intended both for
the offering of incense, and also for sacrifices.

The altars used in the rites of Freemasonry, being Symbolic, combine both
uses. As an altar of sacrifice the candidate
is directed to lay thereon his passions and
vices as an oblation to the Deity, while as
an altar of incense he offers up the thoughts
of a pure heart as incense to Him.

Altars were held peculiarly sacred. They
were places of refuge. Hence we read
" between the horns of the altar," as denoting " Sanctuary," and it was considered an
act of the grossest impiety and sacrilege to
draw any person by violence from it who
sought refuge there.

The presence and use of altars in Masonic
Lodges connect the Institution as a religious
Order with the ancient religious systems.
The contemplative, earnest minded Mason

will ever view the solemn ceremonies employed at the altar, in no other light than
with the most solemn seriousness, and reverence.

The Apron. In Speculative Masonry there
is hardly a more important and more interesting symbol than the Apron. The lesson
it teaches is commenced very early in his
Masonic progress. He will ever remember
that it is the first gift he receives as a Mason,
and he will recall with pride and satisfaction
his consciousness of his being a member of
the Craft. He will remember that it was
the first symbol explained to him. Whatever
may be the depth of the Mysteries into which
he penetrates in his future Masonic career,
and in whatever exalted station his Masonic
zeal and knowledge may place him, he never
parts with "that badge of a Mason" — "The
Lambskin Apron."

In various parts of our ritual we have
references to ancient customs. We may
rest assured that the Apron, too, was
common in all their rites and ceremonies.

The girdle was used among the Israelites
as a part of the dress of the High Priest.

In the mysteries of Mithras the candidate was invested with a white apron. In those of India the candidate received a sash, as a substitute for the apron. The Essenes, as we have before observed, clothed their novices in a white robe. We are informed that the Japanese in certain rites, use a white apron.

"The Apron appears in ancient times to have been an honorary badge of distinction. In the Jewish economy none but the superior orders of the priesthood were permitted to adorn themselves with ornamented girdles which were made of blue, purple, and crimson, decorated with gold, upon a ground of fine white linen, while the inferior priests wore only plain white. The Indian, the Persian, the Jewish, the Ethiopian, and the Egyptian aprons, though equally superb, all bore a character distinct from each other. Some wore plain white ones, others striped with blue, purple and crimson; some of wrought gold, others adorned and decorated with superb tassels and fringes. In a word though the principle honor of the apron may consist in innocence of conduct and purity of heart, yet it certainly appears through all ages to have been a most excellent badge of distinction. In primitive times it was rather an ecclesiastical than a civil decoration; although in some cases the apron was elevated to great superiority as a national trophy. The royal standard of Persia was originally an apron in form and dimensions. At this day it is connected with ecclesiastical honors, for the chief dignitaries of the Christian Church wherever a legitimate establishment with the necessary degree of rank and subordination is formed, are invested with aprons as a peculiar badge of distinction, which is a collateral proof of the fact that Masonry was originally incorporated with the various systems of Divine worship used by every people in the ancient world. Masonry retains the symbol or shadow; it can not have renounced the reality or substance." (Oliver quoted by Mackey.)

There is a legend in the Master Mason's, or the Third Degree of Masonry, which considered as it really is, as a symbol, is "surpassingly beautiful. Let us at once say that there is no historical foundation for this legend. It is in its symbolism we dis-

cern its philosophy. The value of the noble
Institution of Freemasonry to each individual member depends on the *Spirit* in which
its different legends and symbols are understood and treated.

The symbolism of the legend of the conspiracy of the three Assassins is not to be
viewed in any other light but that of a
spiritual signification. Different interpretations of it are held according to the different
views taken of the origin of Speculative
Masonry. Those who give its symbols a
Christian interpretation refer the legend to
the Crucifixion of the Messiah, the type being
the slaying of Abel by his brother Cain.
Those who assign to it a Templar origin refer
it to the conspiracy of the three traitorous
knights who conspired against the Order and
aided King Phillip, styled Phillip the Fair
of France, and Pope Clement the Fifth, to
abolish Templarism and to slay its Grand
Master, Jacques de Molay, in the year 1314.
Those who identify the Craft with ancient
Egyptian Mysteries, as the Germ from which
all the others sprung, interpret the legend as
the symbol of the Evil Principle, or Typhon,

slaying the Good Prince or Siris. In the Philosophic degrees the Myth is interpreted as the war of Falsehood, Ignorance, and Superstition, against Truth.

The Symbolism of the *back* is one of the most important in the whole system of Freemasonry.

We quote Oliver in this connection: "It is a duty incumbent on every Mason to support a brother's character in his absence equally as though he were present, not to revile him *behind his back*, nor suffer it to be done by others, without using necessary attempt to prevent it." Hutchinson, another Masonic writer says in reference to the same symbol: "The most material part of that brotherly love which should subsist among Masons is that of speaking well of each other to the world; more especially is it expected of every member of this Fraternity that he should not traduce a brother. Calumny and slander are detestable crimes against society. Nothing can be viler than to traduce a man *behind his back;* it is like the villainy of an assassin who has not virtue enough to give his adversary the means of self-defense, but lurking in darkness, stabs him whilst he is unarmed and unsuspicious of an enemy."

Beauty is a mark of design in the works of the Creator. Everything we have would equally subserve the wants of man if clothed in a homely garb. It is said to be symbolically one of the supports of the Lodge. The Corinthian column being the most beautiful of the three orders of ancient architecture represents it. The Junior Warden also represents it, as symbolizing the Meridian Sun. Hiram Abif is also represented by the column of beauty, as the beauty of the Temple decoration is attributed to him.

The Blazing Star is a very important symbol in Freemasonry. "It is the first and most exalted object that demands our attention in the Lodge." It is a very ancient symbol, and is frequently used as a Masonic emblem. Much difference of opinion exists as to its true interpretation. This, however, exists mainly as to its signification in the First Degree. In the higher a general uniformity of meaning is preserved.

In the Fourth Degree of the Ancient and Accepted Scottish Rite the star is a symbol of the light of Divine Providence pointing out the way of Truth

In the Ninth Degree it is called "the Star of Direction," as an emblem of the guiding care of God through life's journey.

In the Twenty-eighth Degree the explanation is, that it is symbolic of a true Mason who perfects himself in the way of truth; that is, by advancing in knowledge, becomes like a blazing star shining with brilliancy in the midst of darkness. In this degree the Blazing Star is an emblem of Truth.

In Ancient Craft Masonry we do not find the like uniformity of application. It is not found mentioned in the ritual earlier than the year 1735. The explanation of it as given is, "the Mosaic pavement is the ground floor of the Lodge, the Blazing Star the centre, and the indented tarsel the border round about it."

In certain lectures adopted by the Grand Lodge subsequent to this time, the Blazing Star represented "the Star which led the wise men to Bethlehem proclaiming to mankind the nativity of the Son of God, and here conducting our spiritual progress to the author of our Redemption."

In the Prestonian Lecture it is explained thus: "The blazing star of glory in the center reminds us of that awful period when the Almighty delivered the two tables of stone containing the Ten Commandments to his faithful servant Moses, on Mount Sinai, when the rays of His Divine glory shone so bright that none could behold it without fear and trembling. It also reminds us of the Omnipresence of the Almighty overshadowing us with His Divine love, and dispensing His blessings among us; and by its being placed in the center it further reminds us, that wherever we may be assembled together, God is in the midst of us, seeing our actions and observing the secret intents and movements of our hearts."

Hutchinson explains it after this manner: "It is placed in the center of the lodge, ever to be present to the eye of the Mason, that his heart may be attentive to the dictates and steadfast in the laws of Prudence — for Prudence is the rule of all virtues; Prudence is the path which leads to every degree of propriety; Prudence is the channel whence self-approbation flows forever, she leads us forth to worthy actions, and as a blazing star, enlighteneth through the dreary and darksome paths of this life."

The Continental Masons say of this symbol: "It is no matter whether the figure of which the Blazing Star forms the center be a square, triangle or circle, it still represents the Sacred Name of God, as an universal spirit who enlivens our hearts, who purifies our reason, who increases our knowledge, and who makes us wiser and better men."

In the Lectures adopted by the Grand Lodge of England the following occurs: "The Blazing Star, or glory in the center, refers us to the Sun, which enlightens the earth with its refulgent rays, dispensing its blessings to mankind at large, and giving light and life to all things here below."

The symbolism generally adopted in this country refers to Divine Providence.

We have said that it is a symbol of great antiquity. Let us consider what was its meanings by those ancients who first used it as a symbolism. The worship of the heavenly bodies was one of the first forms of idolatry. Sabaism, or the worship of the Stars, constituted a part of this worship. It was a very general idolatry, arising most probably from the almost universal belief that each star was animated by the soul of a god who had once dwelt as man on the earth. From this circumstance it is that the hieroglyphics represent each star as denoting a god. The language of the prophet Amos elucidates the above statements when he upbraids them as follows for their idolatrous propensities: "But ye have borne the tabernacle of your Moloch and Chium your images, the star of your god, which ye made to yourselves."

Sabaism was early received by the Israelites from the Egyptians. There is evident allusion to this idolatry in the command of God issued through Moses, "Anything that is in the heaven above." The planet Saturn would seem to be the star most generally worshipped under different names by different nations. By the neighboring nations to the Jews it went under the name Moloch, and by the Israelites, themselves, in the wilderness Chium. It is considered to have been peculiarly an Egyptian idolatry. Travelers tell us that at Kibroth Hataavah (graves of lust), in the neighborhood of Sinai, where are found sculptures, at their cemeteries there are numerous representations in hieroglyphics of the star with a human body and a dog's head — the "dog-star."

No matter what theories may have been advanced by writers as to the meaning of the Blazing Star, there is no question but that both in the ancient symbolism, and in Masonry generally, it was the symbol of God, and with the letter G in the center denotes Divine Providence.

"*Blue*" is emphatically and appropriately the color of ancient Craft Masonry. It symbolizes universal friendship and benevolence, because it is the vault of heaven. Among the Jews, blue was used extensively in different parts of their temple furnishings. The word used to express the color signified *perfection*. Among the ancients, initiation to the mysteries and perfection were used synonymously. Not only by the Jews, but also by the Gentiles, blue held a prominent place as a symbolism. With the Druids it was the symbol of *truth;* the candidate into their mysteries was clothed with a robe of white, blue and green.

The ancient Egyptians, the Babylonians, the Hindoos, and the Chinese, represented their gods as clothed in blue.

By Christians in the Middle Ages, the color was considered an emblem of immortality. "The color of the azure was in divine language the symbol of eternal truth; in consecrated language, of immortality; and in profane language, of fidelity."

In the higher degrees of Ancient Scottish Masonry it is used symbolically, and represents universal friendship and benevolence.

"*Burning Bush.*" In the third chapter of the Book of Exodus we read that while Moses kept the flocks of his father-in-law, Jethro, on Mount Horeb, the angel of the Lord appeared to him out of the midst of a bush which burned but was not consumed, and communicated to him the Ineffable Name. In all the ancient Mysteries fire was universally adopted as an emblem of

Deity. From the burning bush came forth the Tetragrammaton, the symbol of Divine light and truth. In the higher degrees it is considered the great source of Masonic light, like the " Orient" is considered in the lower.

Clouded Canopy, or star-decked heaven, is an important and "fundamental symbol in Freemasonry." In the York Rite the clouded canopy is described as the covering of the lodge. Krause, the German writer, says: "That this is to teach us that the primitive lodge is confined within no shut up house, but that it is universal and reaches to heaven, and especially teaching that in every clime under heaven Freemasonry has a seat."

It appears from this that the German interpretation of the symbol differs from the York and American rites, which symbolizes the universality of Freemasonry by the form and extent of the lodge.

The clouded canopy as the covering of the lodge would seem to teach the *aspiration* for a higher sphere.

THE CHISEL. In the English ritual the

Chisel is symbolized as one of the working tools of an Entered Apprentice's degree. "The Chisel demonstrates the advantages of education and discipline. The mind, like the diamond in its original state, is unpolished, but as the effects of the Chisel on the external coat soon presents to view the latent beauties of the diamond, so education discovers the latent virtues and draws them forth to range the large field of matter and space, in order to display the summit of human knowledge — our duty to God, and to man."

CLEAN HANDS. The washing of the hands is an outward sign of an inward purification. The Psalmist says: "I will wash my hands in innocency;" again, "Who shall ascend unto the hill of the Lord, or who shall stand in his holy place? Even he who hath clean hands and a pure heart." In the Ancient Mysteries the washing of hands preceded the ceremony of initiation, and symbolically indicated the purification of the heart from sin as a qualification for those who sought to be initiated. In reference to this idea there appeared an inscription on a temple in the Island of Crete (Candia) in the following words: |"Cleanse your feet, wash your hands, and then enter|" The washing of hands was not only a symbol of purity, but a sacred religious rite among the Ancients. Also among the Hebrews, as we know that at one period of their history even to eat with unwashen hands was a gross violation of custom. A notable instance of this symbolism is that when Pilate sat on the judgment seat and yielded to the demand of the Jews to crucify Jesus, appearing before the people, took water, washed his hands, saying, "I am innocent of the blood of this just man, see ye to it." The white gloves worn by Masons alludes to this symbolism of clean hands.

Corn, Oil, and *Wine* are symbols of the highest antiquity, and in Freemasonry are elements of concentration. In Eastern countries they formed the wealth of the people, and constituted their support. David enumerates them as forming the greatest temporal blessings. \"*Wine* that maketh glad the heart of man and *Oil* to make his face shine, and *Bread* which strengtheneth man's heart.*)'   Both among the Jews and Christian Churches, oil was used in the ceremony of consecration.

The tabernacle in the wilderness, Aaron and his Sons for the priesthood, the high priest, the King, the prophet, altars, etc., were set apart by using the ceremony of annointing with oil.

Freemason's Lodges, which are temples to the Most High, are consecrated to their uses by the ceremony of strewing corn, wine, and oil, upon the "Lodge," which is the emblem of the Holy Ark. The philosophy of this ceremony and symbolism is in the instruction it imparts, "to be nourished with the hidden manna of righteousness, to be refreshed with the Word of the Lord, and to rejoice with *Joy* unspeakable in the richness of Divine grace."

"Wherefore, do you carry *corn, oil,* and *wine* in your processions but to remind you that in the pilgrimage of human life, you are to impart a portion of your *bread* to feed the hungry, to send a cup of your *wine* to cheer the sorrowful, and to pour the healing *oil* of your consolation into the wounds which

sickness hath made in the bodies, or afflic-
tion rent in the hearts of your fellow-trav-
elers." (Harris, quoted by Mackey.)

CORNER STONE in Masonic buildings is
always placed in the northeast corner. By
Operative Masons it is considered the most
important stone in the edifice, because it is
that on which it is supposed the whole foundation rests. In ancient as well as in modern times foundation stones were laid with
important ceremonies.

In the Masonic rites the Symbolism of the
corner stone is very significant. The *form*
of the stone must be square, and yet the
stone itself must be a cube in respect to its
solid contents. The philosophy of this
is that "the square is a symbol of morality, and the cube of truth It lies
between the North, the place of darkness, and the East, the place of light,
and in this situation symbolizes the
Masonic progress from darkness to light, and
from ignorance to knowledge. The perma-
nence and durability of the corner stone,
which lasts long after the building in whose
foundation it was placed has fallen into decay,

is intended to remind the Mason that, when
this earthly house of his tabernacle shall
have passed away, he has within him a sure
foundation of eternal life — a corner-stone of
immortality — an emanation from the Divine
Spirit which pervades all nature and which,
therefore, must survive the tomb and rise
triumphant and eternal above the decaying
dust of death and the grave."

If you have ever seen a foundation stone
laid with Masonic ceremonies, you will
observe that when it is placed in its proper
position it is carefully examined by the working tools of the Operative Mason — the
square, the level, and the plumb.   In Speculative Masonry these are all Symbolic.
When the stone is laid the formula is used
pronouncing it, "Well-formed, true, and
trusty."   In this manner the Mason is
taught, that he is to be "tested by temptation
and trial, by suffering and adversity before
he can be pronounced by the Master builder
of Souls to be materials worthy of the Spiritual building of eternal life, fitted as living
stones for the house not made with hands,
eternal in the heavens."

He will also observe that in the ceremony the corn, oil, and wine, the elements of the Masonic consecration, are produced, and poured on it. This is emblematic of the Nourishment, Refreshment, and Joy which are to be the rewards of a faithful performance of duty.

The Christian Evangelists use it symbolically in reference to Christ — the "Chief Corner Stone." In the Symbolism of Freemasonry, it signifies a true Mason, and is the Character that is first presented to the Apprentice after the completion of his initiation.

DARKNESS in Freemasonry is a Symbol of ignorance. It is held "that the eye should not see until the heart has conceived the true nature of those beauties which constitute the Mysteries of the Order."

In the Ancient Mysteries, previous to initiation, the candidate was placed in a position of darkness until the communication of the light of knowledge was granted him. Various periods of preparatory darkness was imposed on the aspirants of the different Mysteries. With the Druids of Britain the period was nine days and nights ; among the Greeks it was twenty-seven days, and it is asserted that among the Persians that fifty days of darkness, combined with fasting and solitude, were required.

The Bible informs us that darkness prevailed before light, \"And God said let there be light and there was light,\' denoting evidently that darkness existed previous to the giving of light. In Freemasonry darkness represents preparation. In the Symbol of the chaotic state in which the world was before light was brought forth by the Divine command.

The candidate for Freemasonry is in a state of darkness until he receives the light of the Truth imparted to him. Darkness, too, may be considered as a symbol of death, and the imparting of light as a symbol of the glory of the Eternal vision of life everlasting.

DEATH. The Scandinavians describe death in their Eddas in the gloomiest manner imaginable. The ancient heathen generally believed in annihilation. The Ancient Mysteries, however, were based on the doctrine of the immortality of the soul. The Masonic teaching points to it as the gate to which entrance into immortal life is obtained. The Masonic and the Christian idea of death agree in investing it with no gloomy forebodings. They represent it as a sleep from which there is an awakening into another life. "The maid is not dead, but sleepeth," "Our friend Lazarus sleepeth," were uttered by our Saviour in reference to death.

The philosophy of the Third Degree is to teach the Resurrection of the body and eternal life. "Life here is the time of labor, and working at a Spiritual Temple, we are worshipping the Grand Architect for whom we built that Temple. But when life is ended, it closes only to open upon a newer and higher one, where in a second Temple and a purer Lodge, the Mason will find eternal truth. Death, therefore, in Masonic philosophy, is the symbol of initiation completed, perfected, and consummated."

The EAST was always considered sacred by the Ancients. In the earliest sacred rites the sun was an object of worship. When he arose to commence the day in the east they associated this point with his birthplace. Among the Hebrews the east was looked upon with reverence.\ The camp of the tribe of Judah was placed in the east as a mark of distinction.\ The tabernacle in the wilderness was placed due east and west.\ This practice is continued in some of the Christian churches. The practice of the primitive Christians and of some branches of the Christian church is still to turn to the East in their devotions. Masonic lodges, too, are built with an east and west position.

The Orientation of the early Christians is accounted for by St. Augustine in the following words: \"Because the East is the most honorable part of the world, being the region of light whence the glorious sun arises.\"\ In the old lectures the Mason was represented as traveling from West to East; that is, from darkness to light.

The East is the place where the Master sits, and is always considered the most honorable and distinguished. A Masonic writer says: "The veneration which Masons have for the East confirms the theory that it is from the East that the Masonic cult proceeded, and that this bears a relation to the primitive religion whose first degeneration was sun worship."

The KEY in the old rituals was considered one of the most important symbols, and signifies to every brother the importance of keeping the tongue of good report, and to abstain from the contemptible and debasing vices of slander and defamation. It was the symbol of silence and prudence among the ancients, and especially is mentioned so by Greek writers.

In the Mysteries of Isis it was hieroglyphically employed to denote the opening of the heart and conscience in the realm of death for trial and judgment.

As a symbol it is equivalent to the instructive tongue, at least in the Fellow Craft's Degree. It is a significant and appropriate custom in Germany, which might also be profitably followed elsewhere, to make the key a part of the Masonic clothing, to remind each brother that he should lock up or conceal the secret of Freemasonry in his heart, and that he should speak well of a brother in his absence as well as in his presence.

The key also was a symbol of power. It was an ancient custom to give the keys of the house to the newly-made bride, to show her authority over the household. In like manner it is employed in Scripture. The prophet Isaiah says: "The key of the house of David will I lay upon his shoulders, so he shall open and none shall shut, and he shall shut and none shall open," and our Saviour expressed a similar idea when he said to Peter, "I will give unto thee the keys of the kingdom of heaven."

KEY-STONE is that which is placed in the centre of an arch and establishes it in permanency and security. We owe it to the researches of modern archæologists to show that the accusation of anachronism as to the existence of knowledge of arches in the days of King Solomon was groundless. Wilkinson discovered arches with regular key-stones in the doorways of the tombs of Thebes. These are supposed to have been built in the year 1540 B. C., or 460 years before the building of King Solomon's Temple. Other authorities state that arches have been discovered which date from a period as remote

as Abraham. There is every reason to believe that the Dionysian Architects were
acquainted with the construction of arches
in the time of King Solomon, and it is supposed some of them were employed in the
building of the Temple.

LABOR is one of the most important words
in the system of Freemasonry. It is certainly one of the beautiful and commend-
atory features of the Order. It embraces in
its meaning the whole legitimate work of
the Lodge. This term of the Operative
Craft is used symbolically in Speculative
Masonry. \The Operative Masons were engaged in building material edifices, the
Speculative are employed in building spiritual ones. "To labor is to pray," or "labor
is worship." This estimate of labor has
been always a prominent feature of Freemasonry, and no other *human* society under
heaven so prominently sets it forth. Free
and Accepted Masons are constantly employed in rearing a temple whose foundation
is belief in God, and the superstructure is
virtue, morality, and that social feeling which
teaches and emphasizes brotherly love. Our

work is not a building made with hands,
which in time will perish, but ours is imperishable and lasting as eternity. We have
the evidence of our work in our own conscience, and this internal consciousness will
either accuse or else commend us. If our
conscience commend us, then, when this
house of our earthly pilgrimage is dissolved,
we shall receive the invitation: "Well done,
good and faithful servant, enter thou into
the joy of thy Lord" and enjoy thy eternal
reward.

JACOB'S LADDER. We trace this symbolism to Jacob's vision at Bethel when he
was journeying to Padanaram to sojourn
with his uncle Laban. This is related in the
twenty-eighth chapter of the Book of
Genesis. When sleeping one night with a
stone for his pillow, he had a vision of a
ladder whose foot rested on earth, and its
top reached to heaven. On this he saw
the Angels of God ascending and descending. God promised him the blessings which
had been promised to Al.aham, and to his
father Isaac. On awakening Jacob said:
"This is none other than the House of God

and the Gate of Heaven," and he consecrated the place, calling it Bethel, or the
House of God.

This ladder has its analogy in the initiations of the Ancient Mysteries. It was
universally used to symbolize intellectual
and moral progress. Usually the number of
the rounds of the ladder was *seven*, because
of its mystical character. These were
called steps, degrees, or gates. In the
Persian Mysteries of Mithras the number
was seven, and symbolized the soul's approach to perfection.

In Brahmanism a reference is made to the
ladder of seven steps, and the universe was
symbolized by them. The ascent of the
ladder was emblematic of a change from a
lower to a higher sphere of existence — from
death to life, from time to eternity.

In Freemasonry the ladder is presented to
us in the symbolism of the first degree.
The steps are Temperance, Fortitude, Prudence, Justice, Faith, Hope, and Charity its
principal rounds being the three last mentioned.

Different interpretations have been given

of the ladder.	Mackey quotes a writer of
the sixteenth century who says that ".Jacob's
ladder is a symbol of the progressive scale
of intellectual communication betwixt earth
and heaven; and upon the ladder, as it were,
step by step, man is permitted with the
angels to ascend and descend until the mind
finds blissful and complete repose in the
bosom of divinity.	The highest step being
theology or the study and contemplation of
the Deity in His own abstract and exalted
nature."

Another writer says that Luz (the ancient
name of Bethel), was Mount Moriah and that
the place where the ladder rested afterwards
became the Holy of Holies, and was a prophetic symbol of the Temple.

Another interprets it as the prayers of
man and the answering inspiration of God.

In some of the Masonic lectures the ladder is supposed to rest on the Holy Bible
and to reach to heaven.	The Symbolism is
then explained.

"By the doctrines contained in the Holy
Bible we are taught to believe in the Divine
dispensation of Providence, which belief

strengthens our *Faith*, and enables us to ascend the first step.

"That faith naturally creates in us a *Hope* of becoming partakers of some of the blessed promises therein recorded, which Hope enables us to ascend the second step.

"But the third and last being *Charity* comprehends the whole, and he who is possessed of this virtue in its ample sense, is said to have arrived to the summit of his profession, or more metaphorically, into an ethereal mansion veiled from the mortal eye by the starry firmament."

MOSAIC SYMBOLISM. In no religion professed by mankind has symbolism been such a prominent feature as that of the Mosaic. An underlying system of symbolism pervades every part of it from the tabernacle to the smallest article employed in its services. The whole of the Jewish ritual, described so minutely in the Pentateuch, was symbolic. Long before the time of Pythagoras the Mystical nature of numbers was taught by Moses, and even the name of God "was constructed in symbolic form to indicate His eternal nature."

The fringes of the garments were used, not for ornament, but that they might "remember all the commandments of the Lord and do them." An estimate of this symbolism is given thus. "In the symbolism of the Mosaic worship it is only ignorance that can find the details trifling or the descriptions minute, for if we recognize the worth and beauty of symbolism we shall in vain seek in the Mosaic symbols for one superfluous enactment or one superstitious idea."

Freemasonry has derived much of its symbolism from the Mosaic system. Naturally, then, its symbolism is considered by us very significant. Except in the higher degrees we may say that all the symbolism of Masonry is derived from the Jewish. The symbolism of the Temple is constantly used by us, and comes to us from the Tabernacle. In the traditions of Freemasonry King Solomon is revered as their Grand Master because the Temple he erected was the symbol of the Divine life to be cultivated in every heart. The idea of the Jews that every Hebrew should be a temple to the Lord has been transmitted

through the Masonic system which teaches
that every Mason should, by the purity of
his thoughts and life, be a Temple to the
Great Architect.

"Most of the symbology of the Christian
Church was derived from the ancient
Romans. All the higher degrees of Masonry
partaking of a Christian character are
marked by Roman symbology transmuted
into Christian. But Craft Masonry more
ancient and more universal, finds its symbolic teachings almost exclusively in the
Mosaic symbolism instituted in the wilderness.

LIGHT in what we may call the emblematic blazonry of nature, is the emblem of
truth. The sun sustaining a relation to the
natural world is designed by analogy to
that of God in the moral universe. "God is
a sun," "God is light and in Him is no darkness at all." As all light emanates from the
sun so all truth proceeds from God. As
light is adapted to the eye so is truth to the
mind. That this analogy is not fanciful but
is the necessary result of a law of nature,
appears from a fact that in all languages light

is used as the synonyme of truth. Nor is it ever conceivable that a language should be framed in which darkness should be made the emblem of truth, and light the emblem of falsehood. Starting from the sun and tracing out the analogy in various directions, we find that all nature is really emblematic — a vast complex analogon of the spiritual universe, and as this could not be by chance, so we are distinctly assured *it was by design.* And God said * * * "Let them be for signs and for seasons, etc."

Light is represented in Scripture as the immediate result and offspring of the Divine command. \ God said: "Let there be light, and there was light.'\ Hence the origin of light as of every other part of the universe is referred to the exertion of the Divine will. The narrative in the original is so simple, yet so impressively majestic both in thought and diction, that our hearts are filled with a lofty sentiment of wonder and awe. All the enjoyments of life were used under the imagery of light. The transition was natural from earthly to heavenly, from corporeal to spiritual things. Light came to typify true religion and the happiness it imparts. But as light not only came from God, but also makes man's way clear before him, so it was employed to signify moral truth, and pre-eminently that Divine system of truth which is set forth in the Bible, from its earliest gleanings onward to the perfect day of the "Great Son of Righteousness" arising with healing in his wings for every human trouble and woe.

In the system of Freemasonry light has a specially significant meaning. It comprehends the very essence of Speculative Masonry. Its meaning is not restricted to *wisdom* or *truth* as we commonly understand them, but embraces all the other symbols of the Order.

LANDMARKS. What is the significance of the command: "Thou shalt not remove thy neighbor's landmark, which they of old time have set in thine inheritance." It refers to the ancient custom of setting up pillars of stone to mark the boundaries of lands. To remove these maliciously was a henious offense. Freemasons are distinguished as the "sons of light." Their order possesses a *universal language* and *universal laws.* These are peculiar features which are designated "landmarks." To remove any of these is considered the gravest offense against Freemasonry.

What are the landmarks of Freemasonry? Much diversity of opinion exists as to what constitutes them. In our opinion they must possess two features — *antiquity* and *universality.* Hence the restricting of them to any loose or general feature of the Order would be misleading and incorrect. Dr. Oliver says that some restrict them to the obligations, signs, tokens, and words, and that others include with these, the ceremonies of initiation, passing and raising, also the characteristic symbols of the ornaments, furniture, and jewels. Some also think that the Order has no secrets beyond its peculiar secrets.

In connection with this we are assured of one fact, and that is that no *modern* customs of the Order can be looked upon in the light of a landmark.

In fact, the safest and best plan would be to consider only those features of the Order.

as landmarks that have an antiquity older than the memory of man or history can reach.

There is one special characteristic of these landmarks — *they can not be repealed.* They are like the "laws of the Medes and Persians that altereth not." What they were centuries ago they still are, and ever will remain until Masonry itself ceases to exist.

Mackey enumerates twenty-five of these which he says are very generally adopted by the Craft. We give a summary of the most prominent of them:

First — The modes of recognition, which are most legitimate and unquestioned, and admit of no variation.

Second — The division of symbolic Masonry into three degrees is a landmark that has been better preserved than almost any other. The spirit of innovation here has left its traces in the disruption of the Third Degree, causing a want of uniformity in the final teaching of the Master's Order; and the Royal Arch of England, Ireland, Scotland and America, are all made to differ in the mode in which they lead the neophyte to the great consummation of all symbolic

Masonry. In the year 1813 the Grand Lodge
of England vindicated the ancient landmark
by solemnly enacting that Ancient Craft
Masonry consisted of the three degrees,
Entered Apprentice, Fellow Craft, and Master Mason, including the Holy Royal Arch.
Though this is acknowledged in its integrity,
still it continues to be violated.

Third — The legend of the Third Degree is
an important landmark; the integrity of which
has been well preserved. This is especially
necessary, as the legend of the Temple
Builder constitutes the very essence and
identity of Masonry.

Fourth — The government of the Fraternity by a presiding officer called a Grand
Master who is elected from the body of the
Craft. Many suppose that the election
of a Grand Master is due to the law of
the Grand Lodge. But this is not so.
The office is indebted to a landmark and
had an existence long prior to the institution of the Grand Lodge. If the Grand
Lodge were abolished still a Grand Master
would be necessary.

Fifth — The prerogative of the Grand
Master to preside over every assembly of the
Craft wherever held. This is an ancient
usage and is not derived from any special
enactment of the Grand Lodge. He is also
entitled to preside at the communication of
every subordinate Lodge where he might
happen to be present.

Sixth — The Grand Master has also the
prerogative of granting dispensations.

Seventh — It is a prerogative of the
Grand Master to make Masons at sight.
This is a landmark, although there has been
much apprehension in regard to it.

Eighth — The necessity for Masons to con-
gregate in Lodges is another landmark. It
must not be understood by this that any
ancient landmark has directed the permanent organizations of subordinate lodges
which constitutes one of the features of the
Masonic system as it now prevails. But the
landmarks of the Order always prescribed
that Masons should, from time to time con-
gregate together for the purpose of either
Operative or Speculative labor, and that
these congregations should be called Lodges.

Formerly these were extemporary called together for a particular purpose and then dissolved.

Tenth — The government of the Craft when so congregated in a Lodge by a Master and two Warden's, is also a landmark. The presence of a Master and two Wardens is as essential to the valid organization of a Lodge as the Warrant of Constitution is at the present day.

Eleventh — The necessity that every Lodge when so congregated should be duly tiled is an important landmark of the Order which is never neglected. The necessity of this arises from its esoteric character. The duty of keeping off cowans and eavesdroppers is an ancient one, which, therefore, constitutes it a landmark.

Twelfth — The right of every Mason to be represented in a general assembly of the Craft and to instruct his representatives is a twelfth landmark. Formerly, these general meetings which were held once a year were called "General Assemblies" to which all members of the Craft, even the Entered Apprentices were invited. Now they are called " Grand Lodges," and only the Masters and Wardens of the Subordinate Lodges are summoned.   But this is as the representatives of their members.   Originally every Mason represented himself.   Now he is represented by his officers.

Thirteenth — The right of every Mason to appeal from the decision of his brethren, in Lodge, convened, to the Grand Lodge or General Assembly of Masons is a landmark highly essential to the preservation of Justice, and the prevention of oppression. A few Modern Grand Lodges in adopting a regulation, that the decision of Subordinate Lodges, in cases of expulsion, can not be wholly set aside upon an appeal, have violated this unquestioned landmark as well as the principles of just government.

Fourteenth — The right of every Mason to visit and sit in every regular Lodge is an unquestionable landmark of the Order   This is called the " right of visitation."   This right is inherent in every Mason as he travels through the world.   Circumstances may forfeit this right, but when a Mason in good standing knocks at the door for admission there should be good and sufficient reason why this landmark should be violated

Fifteenth — It is a landmark of the Order that no visitor unknown to the brethren present, or to some one of them as a Mason can enter a Lodge without first passing an examination according to ancient usage. This landmark refers only to strangers who are not to be recognized unless after strict trial, due examination, or lawful information.

Sixteenth — No Lodge can interfere in the business of another Lodge, nor give degrees to brethren who are members of other Lodges. This is undoubtedly an ancient landmark, founded on the great principles of courtesy and fraternal Kindness, which are at the very foundation of our Institution.

Seventeenth — It is a landmark that every Freemason is amenable to the Laws and Regulations of the Masonic Jurisdiction in which he resides, and this although he may not be a member of any Lodge. Non-affiliation does not exempt a Mason from Masonic Jurisdiction.

Eighteenth — Certain qualifications of candidates for initiation are derived from a landmark of the Order. These are that he shall be a man, unmutilated, free born, and of mature age. These qualifications arise from the very nature of the Masonic Institution, and from its symbolic teachings, and have always existed as landmarks.

Nineteenth — A belief in the existence of God, as the Grand Architect of the Universe is one of the most important landmarks of the Order. It has been always admitted that a denial of the existence of a Supreme and Superintending Power is an absolute disqualification for initiation. The annals of the Order never yet have furnished or could furnish an instance in which an avowed Atheist was ever made a Mason. The very initiatory ceremonies of the First Degree forbid and prevent the possibility of such an occurrence.

Twentieth — Subsidary to this belief in God, as a landmark of the Order, is the belief in a resurrection to a future life. This doctrine runs through the whole symbolism of the Order. To believe in Masonry and not in a resurrection would be an absurd anamoly.

Twenty-first — It is a landmark that a "Book of the Law" shall constitute an indispensable part of the furniture of every Lodge. By the "Book of the Law," is meant that which, according to the religion of the country, is believed to contain the revealed will of the Great Architect of the Universe. Hence, in all Christian countries, the "Book of the Law" would compose the Old and New Testaments. Where Judaism was the prevailing religion the Old Testament alone would be sufficient. Masonry does not interfere with any man's religion. Whatever he believes to be the revealed will of God constitutes his trestle-board and must ever be before him in his hours of speculative labor to be the rule and guide of his conduct.

Twenty-second — The equality of all Masons is another landmark of the Order. This does not interfere with the usages of society in "giving honor to whom honor is due," but it applies that as children of the Great Father in heaven we meet in the Lodge upon the level —|— that on that level we are all traveling to one predestined goal —|— that in the Lodge genuine merit shall receive more respect than boundless wealth, and that virtue and knowledge alone should be the basis of all Masonic honors, and be rewarded with preferment.

Twenty-third — The secrecy of the Institution is another and most important landmark. The form of secrecy is a form inherent in it, existing with it from its very foundation, and secured to it by its ancient landmarks. If divested of its secret character, it would lose its identity, and would cease to be Freemasonry. The landmark stands before us an insurmountable obstacle against any change in its character in this respect. If it were legal to expose it, then social suicide would follow, and the association which has stood for many centuries would not last for so many years. Hence, its secret feature must be preserved inviolate.

Twenty-fourth — The foundation of a Speculative science on an Operative art, and the symbolic use and explanation of the terms of that art for the purpose of religious or moral teaching, constitutes another landmark of the Order. The Temple of Solomon was as the symbolic cradle of the Institution,

and therefore the reference to the Operative
Masonry which constructed that magnificent
edifice, to the materials and implements
which were employed in its construction,
and to the artists who were engaged in the
building, are all component and essential
parts of the body of Freemasonry, which
could not be subtracted from it without an
entire destruction of the whole identity of
the Order.

Twenty-fifth — The last and crowning
landmark of all is, that these landmarks
can never be changed — nothing can be subtracted from them — nothing can be added
to them — not the slightest modification can
be made in them. As they were received
from our predecessors, we are bound by the
most solemn obligations of duty to transmit
them to our successors.

STONE OF FOUNDATION is a deeply significant symbolism in the system of Freemasonry. There are other stones used as
symbols by the Craft, but this is to be distinguished from them. For instance, in the
First Degree there is a beautiful reference
made to the *corner-stone*, whose position was

always in the northeast corner of the building. It is not alone in Masonry that the
Stone of Foundation has its tradition and
symbolism. Jewish, and even Mohammedan
writers refer to it. In Freemasonry it has a
peculiar symbolic meaning.

"The Stone of Foundation is supposed to
have been placed within the foundation of
King Solomon's Temple, and afterwards,
during the building of the second Temple,
was placed in the Holy of Holies. It was in
the form of a perfect cube, and had inscribed
upon its upper face, within a delta or triangle, the sacred tetragrammaton, or ineffable
name of God."

Of course this stone must be viewed only
in the sense of an allegory, and not as
possessing any basis of fact in history.

The Masonic traditions connected with it
are: The Stone of Foundation was possessed by Adam in the Garden of Eden,
and used as an altar. He so reverenced it
that when he was expelled from Eden he
brought it with him.

Another legend says that from Adam the
Stone of Foundation descended to Seth, and

from him in regular succession to Noah, who took it with him into the Ark, and after he came out of it, it was the stone on which he offered his first sacrifice of thanksgiving. Noah left it on Mount Ararat, where it was found by Abraham, who used it in his wanderings constantly as an altar. His grandson, Jacob, took it with him to Padan-aram, and used it as a pillow on the night on which he had his remarkable vision. There is an interruption here of the legendary history, and we have no account of the manner into which it came into the possession of Solomon, excepting that it is said that Moses brought it with him out of Egypt at the time of the Exodus.

There is, however, another, and more generally adopted legend connected with the Stone of Foundation by Freemasons, which is: "Enoch, under the inspiration of the Most High, and in obedience to the instructions which he had received in a vision, built a Temple underground on Mount Moriah, and dedicated it to God. His son, Methuselah, constructed the building, although he was not acquainted with

his father's motives for the erection. This
temple consisted of nine vaults, situated perpendicularly beneath each other, and communicating by apertures left in each vault.

" Enoch then caused a triangular plate of
gold to be made, each side of which was a
cubit long; he enriched it with the most
precious stones, and encrusted the plate
upon a stone of agate of the same form. On
the plate he engraved the true name of God,
or the Tetragrammaton, and placing it on a
cubical stone, known thereafter as the Stone
of Foundation, he deposited the whole
within the lowest arch.

" When this subterranean building was
completed, he made a door of stone, and
attaching it to a ring of iron by which it
might be occasionally raised, he placed it
over the opening of the uppermost arch, and
so covered it that the aperture could not be
discovered. Enoch, himself, was not permitted to enter it but once a year, and on the
deaths of Enoch, Methuselah, and Lamech,
and the destruction of the world by the
deluge, all knowledge of the vault or subterranean temple, and the Stone of Founda-

tion, with the sacred and ineffable name inscribed upon it, was lost for ages to the world."

At the building of the first Temple of Jerusalem, the Stone of Foundation again makes its appearance. Reference has already been made to the Jewish tradition that David, when digging the foundation of the Temple, found in the excavation which he was making a certain stone, on which the ineffable name of God was inscribed, and which stone he is said to have removed and deposited in the Holy of Holies.

The Masonic and Jewish traditions substantially agree, differing only in the one particular of substituting Solomon for David. It is supposed that this stone was the identical one that was deposited by Enoch. Again, it is stated that this Stone of Foundation was removed by King Solomon, and deposited in a safer place. The Masonic tradition agrees with this, the Jewish.

It is stated that "there was a stone in the Holy of Holies, on its west side, on which was placed the Ark of the Covenant, and before, the pot of manna and Aaron's rod.

But when Solomon had built the temple, and foresaw that at some future time it would be destroyed, he constructed a deep and winding vault under ground, for the purpose of concealing the ark, wherein Josiah afterwards, as we learn in the Second Book of Chronicles, xxxv., 3, deposited it with the pot of manna, the rod of Aaron, and the oil of anointing."

This Stone of Foundation is symbolically referred to in several of the Masonic degrees, and prominently sets forth His creative power — the Grand Architect of the Universe. This allegorically connects the work of God as a model with the Mason's erection of a temporal building.

The Mystical Stone was placed in the foundation, by King Solomon, in the first temple; that is, the first temple of our present life must be built on the sure foundation of divine truth. "The foundation stone is concealed in the first temple, and the Mason knows it not. He has not the true word. He receives only a substitute. But in the second temple of the future life, we have

passed from the grave which had been the
end of our labors in the first. We have
removed the rubbish, and thrown away the
substitute for truth which had contented us
in the former temple, and the brilliant efful-
gence of the Tetragrammaton and the Stone
of Foundation are discovered ; and thence-
forth we are the possessors of the true word
— the Divine Truth." And in this way the
Stone of Foundation, or Divine Truth, concealed in the first temple, but brought to
light in the second, will explain that passage
of the Apostle Paul: "Now we see through
a glass darkly, but then face to face; now we
know in part, but then we shall know even
as we are known."

The sum of the matter is, that this Stone
of Foundation is, Masonically, the symbol of
Divine Truth, upon which all Speculative
Masonry is built; "and the legends and traditions which refer to it are intended to
describe, in an allegorical way, the progress
of truth in the soul, the search for which is a
Mason's labor, and the discovery of which is
his reward." The whole, then, is an illustration of that beautiful "science of morality

veiled in allegory and illustrated by symbols."

Pillars of the Porch were erected by King Solomon at the entrance of the porch of the temple. Josephus gives the following account of them: "Moreover, this Hiram made two hollow pillars, whose outsides were of brass, and the thickness of the brass was four fingers' breadth, and the height of the pillars was eighteen cubits, and the circumference was twelve cubits ; but there was cast with each of their chapiters, lily work, that stood upon the pillar, and it was elevated five cubits, round about which there was net work, interwoven with small palms made of brass, and covered the lily work. To this also were hung two hundred pomegranates, in two rows. The one of these pillars he set at the entrance of the porch on the right hand (or *south*), and called it Jachin, and the other at the left hand (or *north*), and called it Boaz."

When Solomon erected these pillars, it is supposed he had in view the two pillars which guided the Israelites in the wilderness — the pillar of cloud by day and the

pillar of fire by night. It certainly can not
have been for mere ornament that Solomon
had them erected; it was to represent and
memorialize the repeated promises of God of
support to his people.

The meaning of the word "Jachin" is,
"God will establish," and of "Boaz," "in
strength shall it be established." Thus they
served as a remembrance to the Jews in passing daily through them, of the great promises
of God, which would raise their heart in devout thankfulness to Him as the Author of
all blessings.

These pillars were situated *within* the
porch, at its entrance, one on each side of
the gate; one on the right hand, the other on
the left. Ezekiel similarly places the pillars
that he saw in the vision of the temple.
"The length of the porch was twenty cubits,
and the breadth eleven cubits, and he brought
me by the steps whereby they went up to it,
and there were pillars by the posts, one on
this side and another on that side."

These pillars are referred to in various
places in Scripture, and, as we have said,
by Josephus. In the Bible they are men-

tioned in the Books of Kings and Chronicles, and the description given of them in these consistently agree with the above.

What is the Masonic symbolism of these pillars? They are found universally diffused through all the rites. This is but natural, for the symbolism of our Order is founded on the Temple of Solomon, and these being an important and significant part of it, would naturally be used as a symbol.

A writer says: "The pillars represented the sustaining power of God. * * * They suggested just ideas of the power of the Almighty, of the entire dependence of man upon Him, the Creator, and doing this, they exhorted all to fear, to love, and to obey Him."

Hutchinson appears to have been the first who introduced the symbolic idea of the pillars into the Masonic system. He says "the pillars erected at the porch of the temple were not only ornamental, but also carried with them an emblematical import in their names: Boaz being, in its literal translation, *in thee is strength;* and Jachin, *it shall be established,* which, by a very natural trans-

position, may be put thus: O Lord, thou art
mighty, and thy power is established from
everlasting to everlasting."

We may then say that the Masonic symbolism of the two pillars is, first in reference
to their names, symbols of *strength* and stability of the institution, and then in reference to the pillars of fire and cloud, they are
symbolic of our dependence on the superintending guidance of the Grand Architect of
the Universe by which alone that strength
and stability are secured.

POINT WITHIN A CIRCLE is a most interesting symbol in Freemasonry. Some lectures tell us that it represents a brother, the
circle the boundary line of his duty to God
and man, and the two perpendicular parallel
lines the patron saints of the Order — St.
John the Baptist and St. John the Evangelist. Whether this is taken or not as its true
symbolism in Freemasonry, we know that it
was, we might almost say, universally adopted
as a symbol in all the ancient mysteries. In
Freemasonry we can, at all events, say that
the Lodge represents the world or the universe, and the Master and Wardens within

it represent the sun in the three positions. This gives us the true interpretation of the Masonic symbolism of the point within the circle. The Master and Wardens are symbols of the sun, the Lodge of the universe, or world, just as the point is the symbol likewise of it, and the surrounding circle of the universe.

SQUARE AND COMPASS is a Masonic symbol of universal recognition. The square is one of the most significant and important of the symbols of the Order. It is the *trying square* of the stonemason, having a plain surface, and extending to an angle of ninety degrees. It is one of the three "great lights" to the Entered Apprentice, to the Fellow Craft it is one of the working tools, and to the Master Mason it is the official emblem of the Master of the Lodge. It is a symbol of morality, and everywhere inculcates this virtue as well as honesty and truthfulness. This application of it has become so proverbial outside of the Order that the colloquial expression "acting on the square" has become synonymous with *dealing honestly*. It was used as a symbol by

Operative Masons. " In the year 1830, the
architect in rebuilding a very ancient bridge
called Baal bridge, near Limerick, in Ireland, found under the foundation stone an
old brass square, much eaten away, containing on its two surfaces the following inscrip-
tion: I WILL STRVE TO LIVE WITH LOVE
AND   CARE   UPON   THE   LEVL — BY   THE
SQUARE, and the date 1517."   (Mackey.)
It is everywhere recognized as a peculiar
characteristic of Freemasonry.

In Masonic symbolism the Square and
Compass refer to the Mason's duty to the
Craft and to himself, and is a badge or token
of the Fraternity.

A Masonic writer speaks of it thus: " The
square and the compass represent the union
of the Old and the New Testaments. None
of the high degrees accept this interpretation, although their symbolism of the two
implements differs somewhat from that of
symbolic Masonry. The square is with them
peculiarly appropriated to the lower degrees
as founded on the Operative art, while the
compass, as an implement of higher character and uses, is attributed to the degrees

which claim to have a more elevated and
philosophical foundation. Thus they speak
of the initiate when he passes from the Blue
Lodge to the Lodge of Perfection, as 'passing from the square to the compass,' to indicate a progressive elevation in his studies.
Yet even in the high degrees, the square and
compass combined retain their primitive signification as a symbol of brotherhood and as
a badge of the Order."

SECRET VAULT. The symbolism of the
Secret Vault is found only in the high
degrees. Dr. Oliver gives the following
general description of it:

"The foundations of the Temple were
opened and cleared from the accumulation
of rubbish, that a level might be procured
for the commencement of the building.
While engaged in excavations for this purpose, three fortunate sojourners are said to
have discovered our ancient stone of foundation, which had been deposited in the Secret
crypt by Wisdom, Strength, and Beauty,
to prevent the communication of ineffable
secrets to profane or unworthy persons.
The discovery having been made known to

the prince, prophet, and priest of the Jews, the stone was adopted as the chief cornerstone of the re-edified building, and thus became, in a new and more expressive sense, the type of a more excellent dispensation. An avenue was also accidentally discovered, supported by seven pair of pillars, perfect and entire, which from their situation had escaped the fury of the flames that had consumed the Temple and the desolation of war that had destroyed the city. The secret vault that had been built by Solomon as a secure depository for certain secrets that would inevitably have been lost without some such expedient for their preservation, communicated with a subterranean avenue with the King's palace; but at the destruction of Jerusalem, the entrance having been closed by the rubbish of falling buildings it had been discovered by the appearance of a keystone amongst the foundations of the Sanctum Sanctorum. A careful examination was then made, and the invaluable secrets were placed in safe custody."

Treating this legend historically the present state of Jerusalem and its environs clearly show that extensive vaults existed in the Holy City, and especially beneath the superstructure of the original Temple of Solomon. Several writers who have examined these vaults speak of them.

After the destruction of Jerusalem by Titus, the Roman Emperor, Hadrian, erected a temple to Venus on the site of the Jewish structure. A Mohammedan Sultan built the present magnificent structure commonly known as the "Mosque of Omar" on the rock which rises in the centre of the mountain and on the exact site of the ancient Temple of Solomon. The author of " Walks about Jerusalem," says of a vault beneath this Mosque: "Beneath the dome, at the southeast angle of the Temple wall, conspicuous from all points, is a small subterranean place of prayer, forming the entrance to the extensive vaults which support the level platform of the Mosque above."

Jewish writers state that the vault referred to above by Oliver, escaped notice at the destruction of Jerusalem in consequence of its being filled with rubbish, and add that Josiah, foreseeing the destruction of the

Temple, commanded the Levites to deposit the Ark of the Covenant in this vault, where it was found by some of the workmen of Zerubbabel at the building of the Second Temple.

From the remotest ages, we are informed, caves or vaults were held in sacred esteem as places of worship. They were either natural caves or were excavated to suit the purposes of the worshippers. It is thought the form of heathen temples, as well as the aisles, naves, etc., of Christian churches, was derived from the religious uses of subterranean caves.

From this we can well understand the practices of the ancient Mysteries of initiation being performed in caves. The great doctrine, as we have before observed, of the Mysteries was the resurrection from the dead, *to die* and *to be initiated* signifies the same thing, therefore it was appropriate that there should be some outward formal resemblance between the grave and the place of initiation. We may here quote Pindar, the ancient Greek poet, who says: " He who descends beneath the hollow earth, having beheld these

Mysteries, is a happy man, for he knows the end as well as the divine origin of life."

In these ancient Mysteries the vault was symbolic of the grave, and initiation of death where Divine Truth was to be found. This idea has been adopted by Freemasonry which "teaches that death is but the beginning of life, and the first temple of our transitory life is *on the surface* and we must descend into the *secret vault of death* before we can find that sacred deposit of truth which is to adorn our second temple of eternal life. It is in this sense of an entrance through the grave into eternal life that we are to view the symbolism of the secret vault." The historical foundation of this allegory may be true or false in fact, in either case the lesson, its symbolism teaches, is the same, exclusive of its historical foundation.

WINDING STAIRS is a symbolism taught in the Degree of the Fellow Craft. The steps of this winding staircase commenced at the Porch of the Temple, that is at its entrance. Mackey, in his "Encyclopedia of Freemasonry" treats of this symbolism in an exhaustive manner from which we take the following: "Nothing is more undoubted in the science of Masonic Symbolism than, that the Temple was the representative of the world purified by the Shekinah, or the Divine Presence. The world of the profane is without the Temple, the world of the initiated is within its sacred precincts. Hence to enter the Temple — to pass within the porch, to be made a Mason, to be born into the world of Masonic light are all synonymous and convertible terms. Here, then, the symbolism of the Winding Stairs begins.

"The Apprentice having entered within the porch of the Temple, has begun his Masonic life. But the first degree of Masonry, like the lesser Mysteries of the ancient systems of initiation, is only a preparation and a purification for something higher. The Entered Apprentice is the Child in Masonry. The lessons which he receives are simply intended to cleanse the heart and prepare the recipient for that mental illumination which is to be given in the succeeding degrees.

"As a Fellow Craft he has advanced another step, and as the degree is emblematic of youth, so it is here that the intellectual education of the candidate begins. And here at the very spot which separates the porch from the Sanctuary, where childhood ends and manhood begins, he finds stretching out before him a winding stair which invites him, as it were, to ascend, and which, as the symbol of discipline and instruction, teaches him that here must commence his Masonic labor — here he must enter upon those glorious though difficult researches, the end of which is to be the possession of Divine Truth. The winding stairs begin after the candidate has passed within the porch and between the pillars of strength and establishment, as a significant symbol to teach him that as soon as he has passed beyond the years of irrational childhood, and commenced his entrance upon manly life, the laborious task of self-improvement is the first duty that is placed before him. He can not stand still if he would be worthy of his vocation; his destiny as an immortal being requires him to ascend, step by step,

until he has reached the summit, where the
treasures of knowledge await him."

In the ancient systems the number of
steps was odd, because they were considered
more perfect than even ones. Throughout
the Masonic system odd numbers are more
generally used. The number of the stairs
was reckoned seven, conveying the idea of
perfection. It must be remembered, however, that the number of the steps and their
division does not affect the symbolism.

"In the Second Degree of Masonry the
candidate represents a man starting forth on
the journey of life with the great task before
him of self-improvement. For the faithful
performance of this task a reward is promised, which reward consists in the development of all his intellectual faculties, the
moral and spiritual elevation of his character,
and the acquisition of truth and knowledge.
Now, the attainment of this moral and intellectual condition supposes an elevation of
character, an ascent from a lower to a higher
life, and a passage of toil and difficulty
through rudimentary instruction to the full
fruition of wisdom. This is, therefore,

beautifully symbolized by the winding stairs at whose foot the aspirant stands ready to climb the toilsome steep, while at its top is placed 'that hieroglyphic bright which none but Craftsmen ever saw,' as the emblem of Divine Truth, and hence a distinguished writer has said that 'these steps, like all the Masonic symbols, are illustrative of discipline and doctrine, as well as of natural, mathematical, and metaphysical science, and open to us an extensive range of moral and speculative inquiry.'

" The candidate, incited by love of virtue and the desire of knowledge, and withal eager for the reward of truth which is set before him, begins at once the toilsome ascent. At each division he pauses to gather instruction from the symbolism which these divisions present to his attention.

" He is instructed in the peculiar organization of the Order of which he has become a disciple.

" We learn from the monuments of antiquity that at the very beginning of his career man began by a Divine instinct (*Revelation* we would say) to make a separa-

tion between things sacred and profane.
Then came the invention of architecture
with all the mechanical arts connected with
it. Then came the science of geometry to
enable the cultivators of land to designate
the limits of their possessions. All these
are claimed as peculiar characteristics of
SPECULATIVE MASONRY, which may be
considered as the type of civilization."

"Excelsior" must be the motto of every
aspirant after the sublime truths of Speculative Masonry. Without this we can not
understand the true symbolism of the winding stairs. But by constantly acting on it a
rich reward awaits those who ascend, and
this reward or wages consists not in money,
nor corn, nor wine, nor oil. All these are
symbols. His wages are Truth, rather that
approach to which is contained in the degree
to which he has attained. The full Truth
he never can obtain here; he gets a *substitute.* It is only when we enter the more
perfect life that this knowledge is to be
attained.

"It is then only as a symbol we are to
study this beautiful legend of the winding

stairs.   It is offered to us as a great philosophical myth with sublime moral teaching.
It is an allegory to teach us the ascent of
the mind from ignorance, through all the
toils of study, and the difficulties of obtain-
ing knowledge, receiving here a little and
there a little, adding something to the stock
of our ideas at each step, until in the middle
chamber of life — in the full fruition of our
manhood — the reward is attained, and the
purified and elevated intellect is invested
with the reward in the direction how to seek
God, and God's Truth; to believe this, is to
believe and to know the true design of
Speculative Masonry."

DEDICATION OF MASONIC LODGES TO
ST. JOHN THE BAPTIST AND ST. JOHN THE
EVANGELIST.   The ancient Pagan nations
dedicated their temples and altars to some
one of their numerous gods.   The people
observed the days of dedication as Festivals.
The Jews dedicated their Temple and Altars
to the One, Eternal God.   We have numerous instances of such dedication mentioned
in the Scriptures.   David, for instance, solemnly dedicated the altar he built on the site

of the threshing floor of Ornan the Jebusite
when the plague which was sent on the land
was stayed. It is held by some writers that
on this occasion he composed the thirtieth
psalm. Nor was dedication confined to
places assigned for the worship of Jehovah
— it was extended to private houses by
prayer, praise, and thanksgiving.

There appears, however, to have been a
distinction among the Jews between dedication and consecration. Sacred things were
both consecrated and dedicated, while profane or secular things were only dedicated.
Consequently dedication was considered a
less sacred ceremony than consecration.

Jewish writers mention five dedications of
their Temple: 1st. That of Solomon's Temple in the year B. C. 1004. 2d. The dedication in the time of Hezekiah, when it was
purified from the abominations of Ahaz, B.
C. 726. 3d. Dedication of Zerubbabel's, B.
C. 513. 4th. That of Judas Maccabæus,
when he expelled the Syrians, B. C. 164.
5th. Dedication of Herod's Temple, B. C. 22.

In the early ages of Christianity, and still
among certain branches of the Christian

Church, the practice was and is observed of consecrating their places of worship to God and dedicating them to some particular Saint.

A like practice prevails in the Masonic Institution. Whilst Lodges are consecrated "to the honor of God's glory," they are dedicated to the two Saints John — viz., St. John the Baptist, whose festival is held on the 24th of June, and St. John the Evangelist, whose festival occurs on the 27th of December, as our patrons.

It appears that among the early Masons that it was St. John the Baptist, and not St. John the Evangelist, that was adopted as the patron of the Craft.

The Charter of Cologne says: "We celebrate annually the memory of St. John, the forerunner of Christ and the patron of our community."

A Masonic writer says: "The stern integrity of St. John the Baptist, which induced him to forego every minor consideration in discharging the obligations he owed to God; the unshaken firmness with which he met martyrdom rather than betray his duty to his Master; his steady reproval of vice and continued preaching of repentance and virtue, make him a fit patron of the Masonic Institution."

There must be something significant in the connection of St. John the Evangelist with Freemasonry, and some particular reason why he has been adopted as one of the patrons of the Institution. Why was he selected rather than any other of the Evangelists? Was there nothing in his life and writings which drew him very near to Freemasonry? By this we do not mean Freemasonry as we now have it, but something which was very similar to it. Yes, there existed a society of mystical philosophers called the Essenes, who were supposed, as we have already observed, to have derived their origin from the same source as the Freemasons. Several writers assert that St. John belonged to this Fraternity, and that his writings partake of the spirit of their mysticism.

Another reason, however, may be assigned why St. John was selected as the patron of the Order. In comparing the writings of the Evangelist and the tenets of Freemasonry, we see they are similar. There is also a striking similarity between the "Book of the Revelation," in some of its mechanical features, and the Ancient Mysteries. This leads us strongly to the presumption that St. John must have been an initiate of the Association of the Essenes.

The author of "Origin of the Pagan Idolatry" says that "the whole machinery from beginning to end of the Apocalypse seems very plainly to have been borrowed from the machinery of the Ancient Mysteries; and this, if we consider the nature of the subject, was done with the very strictest attention to poetical decorum.

"St. John himself is made to personate *an aspirant* about to be initiated; and, accordingly, the images presented to his mind's eye closely resemble the pageants of the Mysteries both *in nature* and *in order* of *succession.*

"The prophet first beholds a door opened in the Magnificent Temple of heaven; and into this he is invited to enter by the voice of one who plays *the hierophant.* Here he witnesses the unsealing of a *Sacred book,* and forthwith he is appalled by a troop of *ghastly apparitions* which flit in horrid succession before his eyes. Among these are pre-eminently conspicuous a *vast serpent*, the well-known symbol of the great father, and the two portentious *wild beasts*, which severally come up out of the sea and out of the earth. * * *

"Passing these terrific monsters in safety, the prophet, constantly attended by his *angel hierophant*, who acts the part of an interpreter, is conducted into the presence of a *female* who is described as closely resembling the great mother of heathen theology. * * * * On her forehead the very name MYSTERY is inscribed; and the label teaches us that, in point of character, she is *the great universal mother of idolatry.* * * * *

"At length, however, *the first or doleful part* of these Sacred Mysteries draws to a close, and *the last or joyful part* is rapidly approaching. After the prophet has beheld the enemies of God plunged into a dreadful lake or inundation of liquid fire, which corresponds with the infernal lake or deluge of the Orgies, he is introduced into a *splendidly*

illuminated region, expressly adorned with
the characteristics of that Paradise which
was the ultimate scope of the ancient aspirants; while *without* the holy gate of admission are the whole multitude of the profane,
dogs, and *sorcerers,* and *whoremongers,* and
murderers, and *idolators, and whosoever lov-
eth and maketh a lie.*"

"In this imagery of the Apocalypse we
see a close resemblance between the form of
it and that of the Mysteries, and the intimate connection between their system and
that of Freemasonry led our ancient brethren
to claim the patronage of an apostle so pre-
eminently mystical in his writings, and whose
last and crowning work bore so much of the
appearance, in an outward form, of a ritual
of initiation."

THE CROSS. In the Halliwell manuscript
of the Fourteenth Century the cross is referred to as the *rood* or *rode.* There appears
to be no symbolism of it in the first three
degrees of Ancient Craft Masonry. In the
higher degrees, however, it forms an important symbol. In the Rose Croix and Kadosh
it is certainly a representation of the Cross

of Christ. In other degrees, which are of a
philosophical character, the symbolism of the
cross would appear to be borrowed from the
usages of the ancients; because in all countries, even from the earliest times, the cross
has been employed as a sacred symbol.

It is found depicted in the oldest monuments of Egypt, Assyria, Persia, and Hin-
doostan. It certainly was used as a symbol
throughout the Pagan world long before it
became an object of veneration to Christians.

As a symbol used by the ancients it
denoted eternal life. It is stated by a certain writer in treating of the Sign of the
Cross, that in the very earliest epochs of
time there were three principal symbols of
universal use; viz., the *Circle*, the *Pyramid*,
and the *Cross*.

The Celts frequently adopted, in the construction of their Temples, the crucial form.

Another writer says: " The Druids seek
studiously for an oak tree, large and hand-
some, growing up with two principal arms in
the form of a cross, besides the main upright
stem. If the two horizontal arms are not
sufficiently adapted to the figure they fasten

a cross beam to it. This tree they consecrate in this manner. Upon the right branch
they cut in the bark, in fair characters, the
word HESUS ; upon the middle or upright
stem the word TARAMIS; upon the left
branch, BELENUS; over this, above the
going off of the arms, they cut the name of
God, THAU. Under all the same repeated,
THAU. This tree, so inscribed, they make
their *Kebla* in the grove, cathedral, or sum-
mer church, towards which they direct their
faces in the offices of religion."

IMMORTALITY. We have before stated immortality was the prominent lesson taught in
the Ancient Mysteries. No matter how they
may differ in their views concerning it, all
nations, with whose religions we are acquainted, were believers in it. "Without
belief in a personal immortality, religion is
surely like an arch resting on one pillar, like
a bridge ending in an abyss."

The Acacia is used in Freemasonry as the
Symbol of Immortality. It was always considered a sacred plant among the Jews. The
sacred furniture of the Tabernacle was made
from it, such as the Ark of the Covenant, the

table for the Shewbread, etc. In the Scriptures it is called *"Shittim."*

In Freemasonry it is adopted as symbolizing the IMMORTALITY OF THE SOUL. The flower that "cometh up and is cut down" reminds us of the transitory nature of human life, and the evergreen plant reminds us of perpetual youth and vigor. This is beautifully and appropriately compared to our spiritual life in which the soul is freed from the corruptible body, and enjoys an eternal spring. In the impressive funeral services of our Order, these words are used: "This evergreen is an emblem of our faith in the immortality of the soul. By this we are reminded that we have an immortal part within us which shall survive the grave, and which shall never, never, never die." Also, in the lecture of the third degree we are taught that "by the evergreen and ever-living sprig" the Mason is strengthened with confidence and composure to look forward to a blessed immortality; hence the propriety of placing the Sprig of Acacia on the grave of a departed brother to symbolize the incorruptible nature of the soul.

CHAPTER XII.

We have traced all the channels through which, both in ancient and mediæval times, it was possible Freemasonry could come to us. The question still confronts us through which channel are we to trace it to its source? We have seen that there is a striking resemblance between the legends, ceremonies, and myths of the ancient mysteries, and those of the Freemasonry of the present day. We have also seen the singular correspondence, in several of their features, between the Ancient Fraternities of the Roman Colleges of Artificers (who were both Operative and Speculative Masons) — the Religious Fraternities of the Essenes and the Culdees, to the traveling Masons of the Middle Ages, and to the Modern Institutions of Freemasonry.

But is it possible to treat of Freemasonry apart from King Solomon and the Temple he built at Jerusalem? Is not that Temple

itself the great central symbol of the Craft?
And do we not symbolize it in its different
parts? Is it not a fact that from the very
commencement of the foundation to its completion, and the deposit of the Holy Name
in the Sanctum Sanctorum that all was necessary to show forth the great purpose of the
Fatherhood of God and the Brotherhood of
man?

Did not the Temple itself, both as a whole
and in its several parts, symbolize the Universe, which Universe is but a vast Symbol
of the Almighty Architect?

Is it not a fact that if we were to " omit
from our ritual all reference to that sacred
edifice, and to the legends and traditions
connected with it, that the system itself
would at once decay and die, or at best remain only as some fossilized bone, serving
merely to show the nature of the living body
to which it had belonged ?"

Assuredly, we can not treat of the system
of Freemasonry, independent of, or distinct
from, Solomon's Temple; especially, when
we consider the two great divisions into
which modern Freemasonry is divided. The

first of these is that of Master Masons to
whom Solomon's Temple is symbolic of this
present life — which is temporary — fleeting.
The other division is that of the Royal Arch
Masons who go beyond the symbols of Solomon's Temple and its perishable character,
to Zerubbabel's Temple erected on the ruins
of the former. In this second Temple is
seen the Symbol of the life which is imperishable and eternal, and in which the *Truth*
has been found.

Now this brings us to the answer of the
question which we have asked. What is the
origin of Freemasonry? Whence has it
come to us? Calmly investigating the *facts*
of history we have come to the conclusion,
and we have no hesitation in declaring it,
that no one single source can be shown as *the
one* through which the Freemasonry of the
present day has exclusively descended to us.
It is in vain to try to prove that it had its
origin exclusively in the Ancient Mysteries,
nor yet in King Solomon's Temple, neither
has it its origin in the Religious Societies to
which we have referred.

All these had a more or less direct bearing

on each other, from the circumstances that each of them conserved some portions of the truth which mankind had always possessed.

Truth is absolute and eternal. No man can create truth; he can only declare facts out of the great ocean of truth. The centre of all truth is God. He declares Himself to be the truth, when He made the emphatic declaration: "I am the way, the *truth*, and the life," etc. Now, all the systems referred to conserved in their myths, allegories, and symbols, more or less of the truth. In the natural and necessary intercourse of men with their fellows there must be interchange of thought and ideas; and especially on those which affect man as a social and religious being. This inter-communion of sentiments between the members of different associations or Fraternities who may have been contemporaries, must have resulted in at least the partial adoption and modification of the peculiar views of each. When one association preceded the other, then the later would borrow somewhat from the earlier. In this way, especially in the building of Solomon's Temple, Jewish and Tyrian thought had been adopted and modified by each other. So, too, had some of the Early Fathers of the Christian Church adopted some of the thoughts of the heathen philosophers.

We again repeat that there are striking points of resemblance between the Ancient Mysteries and our Freemasonry. We make the same statement in reference to the Roman Colleges of Artificers, the Essenes, the Culdees, the Stone Masons of Germany, and the Companionage of France. All these possess some points of similarity to each other, as well as to Freemasonry; but certainly no one single organization of them can be pointed to as that to which the modern institution of Freemasonry owes its origin. We grant some features of similarity, but we deny that there exists the incontrovertible historical evidence which would prove that the one fraternity or organization merged into the other. We grant the points of similarity, but we deny the *historic continuity*.

Operative Masonry has a very high antiquity, extending to, and antedating the Builders of the Middle Ages. We possess

no historic evidence which unquestionably
assigns to *purely* Speculative Masonry a,
higher date than the Fifteenth Century.
Prior to this time, Operative Masonry possessed but little of the speculative character
of our Freemasonry.

The truth concerning the origin of Speculative Masonry, or the Freemasonry of our
present day, is, that it is the outcome or
development of all the prior organizations.
It has been "evolved" from them.

In the Tenth Century, the Operative Stone
Builders spread all over Europe, and established themselves in England even before
the time of the Norman Conquest. In the
Fourteenth Century, the different trades of
Germany and England formed themselves
into regularly organized bodies, governed by
certain regulations and rules, and were called
"Freemasons." We have historic evidence
that the word "Freemason" occurs as early
as 1350, in the reign of Edward III. The
membership of the different lodges of these
organizations was at first simply operative.
Not until the Fifteenth Century were honorary or non-operative members admitted.

These last included princes, nobles, and high
and learned ecclesiastics. These were styled
"Accepted," and introduced philosophical
and abstract theories into the lodges. The
Operative Art declined after the suppression
of the monasteries and other religious houses
at the period of the Reformation. Practically, the feudal system was also abolished,
and the noble ecclesiastical edifices, episcopal palaces, and baronial piles ceased to be
erected. The Speculative element alone now
preserved the societies of the Operative Art
from utter disintegration and decay. The
Speculative feature became more and more
prominent by the admission of the "Accepted" or honorary members, until at length
the *Operative* feature of the organization
was wholly superseded by the *Speculative*.

About the year 1700, Speculative Masonry
in England began to decline or degenerate
to such an extent as to be used merely for
the purposes of self-interest and gain.

Now commenced the eventful period of
what, in Masonic history, is known as the
" Revival." This period is specially marked
by the formation of the first Grand Lodge in

England, in the year 1717. It appears this Grand Lodge had jurisdiction over most of the European lodges.

For more than one hundred years of the existence of Speculative Masonry the "Masters" had the power of forming Lodges, but this individual power ceased on the formation of the Grand Lodge.

We here inquire what was the scope of the "Revival," and who engaged in it? James Anderson, Minister of a Scottish Presbyterian Church in London, and John Theophilus Desaguliers, of Christ Church, Oxford, assisted by other members of the Fraternity, were commissioned by the rulers of the Order "to peruse and digest into a *new* and *better* method, the History, Charges, and Regulations of the Ancient Fraternity."

Anderson informs us in his "Constitution" published in 1723, "that the brethren revived the drooping Lodges in London." He enters into a fuller and more detailed account in the second edition of the Constitutions published in 1738. The account he gives us in this is the only authentic record we have of the organization formed in 1717.

Preston, the Masonic historian, gives the following account of the transaction:

"On the accession of George I., the Masons in London and its environs, finding themselves deprived of Sir Christopher Wren and their annual meetings discontinued, resolved to cement themselves under a new Grand Master, and to revive the communications and annual festivals of the Society. With this view, the Lodges in London, with some of the old brethren, met in February, 1717, and having voted the oldest Master Mason then present into the Chair, constituted themselves into a Grand Lodge, *pro tempore*, in due form. At this meeting it was resolved to hold Quarterly Communications of the Fraternity, and to hold the next annual assembly and feast on the 24th of June, for the purpose of electing a Grand Master, till they should have the honor of a noble brother at their head. Accordingly on St. John Baptist's day, 1717, in the third year of the reign of King George the 1st, the assembly and feast were held, when the oldest Master Mason, and a Master of a Lodge, having taken the Chair, a list of

proper candidates for the office of Grand
Master was produced, and the names being
separately proposed, the brethren, by a great
majority of hands, elected Mr. Anthony
Sayer, Grand Master for the ensuing year,
who was forthwith invested by the said oldest Master, installed by the Master of the
Oldest Lodge, and duly congratulated by
the Assembly, who paid him homage. The
Grand Master then entered on the duties of
his office, appointed his wardens, and commanded the brethren of the Lodges to meet
him and his wardens, quarterly, in communication, enjoining them, at the same time, to
recommend to all the Fraternity, a punctual
attendance on the next annual assembly and
feast."

At this time a reorganization of the Institution was effected, approved, and accepted
in 1723, becoming known as the "New Constitution." This constitutes the Freemasonry
of the present day so far as it may be looked
upon as an *Organization*. In this reorganization of Freemasonry, sectarianism was
abolished, a universal creed adopted on the
basis of the Fatherhood of God and the

Brotherhood of Man, and a philosophical interpretation given of the ritual and symbols, instead of restricting them exclusively to a particular religious belief. The teaching of Ancient Freemasonry became Cosmopolitan, admitting men of all nationalities, religions, and rank in life, and adopting a philosophy consistent with toleration and universality. But it must be distinctly understood that these broad and liberal principles do not preclude the *Christian* exposition and application of the symbols, ritual, and philosophy of Freemasonry.

Another feature of the reorganization consisted in the adoption of " Degrees." In the original usage of the Craft, there was but the one degree of initiation. This degree included all the elements of what now constitutes the Entered Apprentice, Fellow Craft, and Master Mason. These were simply names of the different classes of workmen. The Fraternity itself was composed of " Fellows." This we can see by consulting the oldest records, constitutions, and charges. We have further testimony of this in the fact that the four old Lodges existing in London in the year 1717 were composed entirely of "Fellows." We can not sufficiently emphasize the fact that, up to the year 1740, there were but three classes, or "Degrees," if we call them so, known in Freemasonry. At that time the "Royal Arch" Degree was evolved from the Third, or Master's Degree. It has been denied by some that the Third Degree had ever been mutilated, but this denial can not be sustained by sufficient evidence; that is, we have no sufficient evidence to prove that it, the Royal Arch, existed prior to 1717.

The Royal Arch does not appear to have been regularly worked in Chapters before 1762, when a Chapter was opened at York, England. It was then known and recognized as the Fourth Degree in Masonry.

"Up to this epoch there were no intermediate degrees. The degree of *virtual* Past Master, or passing the chair of a Lodge, as a qualification, for the Royal Arch, without having been the *actual* Master of a Craft Lodge, was not introduced until 1769, at which time we first hear of the Old Chivalric Order of Knights Templar being associated

with Masonry. This was communicated as
an honorary degree, and recognized by this
Grand Lodge (Grand Lodge of all England)
as the Fifth Degree in Masonry — recorded
as such in 1780 — being the *only* Grand
Lodge that *ever* recognized Templary as
Masonic. *All* these degrees were conferred
under Craft charters, the Masonic . Lodge
being then considered the *only source* of
genuine Freemasonry." (W. J. Bury Mac-
Leod Moore, G. C. Tvc.)

When the Union of the Grand Lodges of
England — the "Ancients" and the "Mod-
erns"— had been effected in the year 1813
(they had been separated since 1751),
the Royal Arch was authorized not as a
separate degree, but as the "Complement"
to the Third, or Master's Degree.

The Royal Arch is very generally diffused
throughout the Masonic world. Because of
its historic and symbolic character, and sublime significance, it has been called the
"Holy Royal Arch." It has also been designated "the root, heart, and marrow of
Masonry." Oliver's testimony of it is, that
"it is indescribably more august, sublime,

and important than any which precede it,
and is, in fact, the summit and perfection of
Ancient Masonry."

As the Master Mason's Degree is now
constituted, we can not fail to see that its
symbolism is in a mutilated condition, being
imperfect and unfinished in its history, and
requiring something to perfect its completion. The Royal Arch supplies what is
wanting. We see then that Ancient Craft
Masonry in its completeness consists of the
three degrees of Entered Apprentice, Fellow
Craft, and Master Mason, with the Holy
Royal Arch. These, and these only, constitute Freemasonry, in the true sense of the
word.

The so-called "High Degrees," notwithstanding their beautiful teaching and sublime
philosophy, had been at first established more
for *class* distinction. They cannot be properly termed *Masonic*. The only legitimate
degrees of Speculative Masonry are the three
degrees above named, with their complement
or completion, the Royal Arch. No matter
how high sounding these titles may be, no
matter how gratifying to our vanity to have

received these "Higher Degrees," we can not ignore the fact that they are extraneous to the "Ancient Free, and Accepted Craft Masonry."

CHAPTER XIII.

A distinguishing feature of Freemasonry lies in the fact that it has in its possession the *historical* records of legends and traditions. This claim is substantiated by documentary evidence. Archæological researches have brought to light several of these documents. And there is reason for the strongest presumption that they are but copies or transcriptions of more ancient documents. These have been styled "The Old Charges of British Freemasons."

Among them are the following:

(1) The "Regius," or "Halliwell" Poem. The date of this is supposed to be the year 1390, and is considered to be the earliest document yet brought to light connected with the progress of Freemasonry in Great Britain. It is not known by whom they had at first been compiled. They are of very great value as containing the records of

Operative Masons. The manuscript is deposited in the British Museum, and is styled "Early History of Freemasonry in England." By J. O. Halliwell, F. R. S., London.

(2) The "Cooke" manuscript. This is deposited in the British Museum, and received its name from the fact of its being edited by Matthew Cooke in the year 1861. It was purchased for the "National Collection" in 1859. Its original cover was of wood which it still has, as well as the rough twine which connects the sheets of vellum on which it is written. The date ascribed to this is the beginning of the Fifteenth century.

(3) The "Landsdowne" manuscript next comes before us. This is published in what is called "Freemason's Magazine." Hughan, the able and indefatigable English Masonic historian has it also in his "Old Charges." This makes a book of seven folios. Many of the principal words are in large letters, and are of an ornamental character. The date assigned to this manuscript is the middle of the sixteenth century.

(4) We treat next of the "Grand Lodge"

manuscript. This is in the possession of the
Grand Lodge of England. It is a parchment
roll, nine feet long, by five inches broad. On
the reverse side of the scroll the first verse
of the first chapter of St. John's Gospel is
written. It was purchased from a descend-
ant of that Thomas Duncherley so conspicu-
ously connected with Freemasonry in the
days of the Revival. The date ascribed to it
is 1583.

(5) Our next manuscript is that styled
"York" No. 1. This is published in "Masonic Magazine," 1873, also in Hughan's
"Old Charges." This is supposed to date
from the 17th century. A "Grand Lodge"
of all England which was held at York, had
five or six of the "Old Charges." An inventory of them was made in 1779, and the following description of No. 1 is given: "A
parchment roll in three slips, containing the
Constitution of Masonry." It was seven
feet in length by five inches in breadth.

(6–7) We have now before us the "Phillips," known also as the "Wilson" manuscript, Nos. 1 and 2. These are written on

vellum. The date assigned to them is the 17th century. They were published in Masonic Magazine, 1876, also in the Archæological Library of 1879. We have the earliest reference to this manuscript in the "Manifesto of the Right Worshipful Lodge of Antiquity" in 1778. The words are: "O. Ms. in the hands of Mr. Wilson, of Broomhead, near Sheffield, Yorkshire, written in the reign of King Henry VIII." This manuscript and a duplicate of it had been missed for a long time, but was discovered by the Rev. A. F. A. Woodford. Mr. Wilson sold them to Sir Thomas Phillips.

(8) "Inigo Jones" manuscript is next before us. This manuscript was published only in the "Masonic Magazine," in the year 1881. The date assigned to it is 1607. It is in the possession of the Provincial Grand Lodge of Worcestershire. It is described as the "Ancient Constitutions of the Free and Accepted Masons." It possesses an ornamental title and drawing by Inigo Jones.

(9) The "Wood" manuscript is our next. This also was published only in the "Masonic

Magazine" of 1881. It is considered a very valuable manuscript, from the fact that it has depicted on the frontispiece masons at work. Its date is 1610. It was obtained from Mr. Wood, who had it in his possession for twenty years. It is written on parchment, and entitled, "The Constitution of Masonrye," wherein is declared the first foundation of divers sciences, and principally the science of Masonry, with divers good rules, orders, and precepts necessary to be observed by all Masons. It is in the possession of the Provincial Grand Lodge of Worcestershire.

(10) This is a parchment roll of Charges on Masonrie, bearing the date 1630. It is the third in the York Inventory of 1779. It is considered to have been a version of the "Constitutions."

(11) The next manuscript is the "Harlein." This is deposited in the British Museum. It is ascribed to the Seventeenth Century. A somewhat incomplete copy of it was published in the "Freemason's Quarterly Review" of 1836. Another copy of it appeared in Hughan's "Old Charges."

(12)   We have another "Harlein" manuscript, whose date is ascribed to the Seventeenth Century also.   It is deposited in the British Museum.   It was published both in the "Masonic Magazine" of 1873 and in "Hughan's Sketches."   This manuscript contains a remarkable obligation "to keep secret" certain words and signs of a Freemason, etc.; also a register of fees paid "for to be a Freemason," etc.   This is considered to be the first mention of "words and signs."

(13)   We have a manuscript which bears the date 1646, called the "Sloane."   It is published in the "Masonic Magazine" of 1873; also in the "Old Charges."

(14)   We have another styled the "Sloane," also which bears the date 1659. This appears in "Hughan's Sketches."   The part relating to "Freemasons" is written on six leaves of paper, 5 inches by 4.

(15)   We now come to a manuscript styled the "Buchanan."   Is deposited in the Freemason's Hall, London.   This was presented to the Grand Lodge of England by Mr. George

Buchanan, in the year 1880. Its probable date is 1680.

(16) We now come to the Kilwinning manuscript. It is deposited in the " Mother Kilwinning " Lodge, Scotland. The date assigned to this is the Seventeenth Century. It was published in "Hughan's Masonic Sketches," and Lyons' History of the Lodge of Edinburg.

(17) " Atcheson Haven " is a manuscript of the date 1666. It is owned by the Grand Lodge of Scotland. This is also called the " Musselburg." It was published in the " History of Freemasonry." A transcript of the original is in the Freemason's Hall, Edinburg. It was printed by Lyon in his history of No. 1, Scotland.

(18) Another manuscript, called the " Aberdeen," bears the date 1670, and is in the possession of the Ancient Lodge of "Aberdeen." It was published in the " Voice of Masonry," Chicago, 1874. The " Laws and Statutes of the Old Lodge of Aberdeen " is first given, then comes the

"Meason Charter," and then the general laws, list of members, etc., beginning 1670.

(19) We now come to a manuscript styled the "Melrose, No. 2," bearing the date 1674. It is in the possession of the Old Lodge of Melrose. It was published in the Masonic Magazine of 1880. It was discovered in 1879, by a Mr. Vernon, of Kelso.

(20) The "Hope" is another manuscript ascribed to the Seventeenth Century. It is in the Lodge of Hope, Bradford, Yorkshire. The title is, "The constitutions, articles, etc., which are to be observed and fulfilled by all those who are made Free by the Rt. Wor. Mrs. Fellowes, and Brethren of Freemasons at any Lodge or Assembly." It was published in "Hughan's Old Charges."

(21) We next notice "York No. 5." This is in the custody of the York Lodge. It is published in the "Masonic Magazine," 1881, from a transcript. It has no date or signature. It is supposed to have been written in the year 1670. It is a roll of paper $7\frac{1}{2}$ feet by 8 inches. It is thought to be a part of another paper Roll of Charges on Masonry.

(22) "York No. 6" is also ascribed to the Seventeenth Century. It was published in the "Masonic Magazine," 1880. It is a parchment Roll of Charges. A part of it was missing, but was subsequently found with the Roll. The concluding portion of the Roll is very significant, containing the following words: "Doe all as ye would bee done unto. And I beseech you at every meeting and assembly you pray heartily for all Christians — Farewell."

(23) The Antiquity Manuscript is in the custody of the Lodge of Antiquity, London. A transcript was made from the original, and published in "Hughan's Old Charges." It is a scroll of parchment 9 feet by 11 inches. It contains, under the arms of the City of London and the Mason's Company, the injunction, "Fear God and keep His Commandments, for this is the whole duty of man." The invocation begins, "In the name of the Great and Holy God." The concluding sentences are, "William Bray, free-man of London, and free-mason."

(24) "Supreme Council No. 1." This

bears the date 1686, and was, but a few years ago, found in Wales, by S. H. Clerke, who presented it to the Supreme Council, 33°, London. The "Old Charges" are written on two parchment skins, sewn together. So far as we know, it has not yet been published.

(25) "York, No. 4." This has been published in Hughan's "Masonic Sketches." It contains the Apprentices Charge. It was presented to the Grand Lodge of York in 1777.

(26) "Alnwick" is a manuscript published in the American edition of "Hughan's Masonic Sketches," 1871. "The Masonic Constitutions," as they are called, are written on the first twelve pages preceding the records of the Company and Fellowship of Freemasons of a Lodge held at Alnwick.

(27) "York, No. 2" now comes before us, and bears the date 1704. It is in the custody of the York Lodge. It was published in Hughan's "Masonic Sketches." It is written on parchment, 60 x 7½ inches. It contains the "Constitutions of Masonrie."

(28) The "Scarborough" is a manuscript

which begins the date 1705, and is in the custody of the Grand Lodge of Canada. It was published in the " Mirror and Keystone," Phil., 1860. It contains the following record: " We .·. .·. that att a private Lode held att Scarborough in the County of York, the 10th day of July 1705 before William Thompson Esqrs P'sident of the said Lodge, and several others brethren, Free-Masons, the several p'sons whose names are hereunto subscribed were then admitted into the said Fraternity."

(29) " Papworth " is a manuscript in the custody of Mr. Wyatt Papworth, London, and bears the date 1714. It was published in " Hughan's Old Charges." It appears to have been formerly in the shape of a roll written on pages of foolscap size which were continuously joined together. The motto in the beginning of the roll is, " In God is all our trust."

(30) We now mention a manuscript styled " Gateshead," in the custody of the Lodge of " Industry," Gateshead. It bears the date 1730. It was published in the " Masonic Magazine." The oldest minutes

in this manuscript were bound up with a copy of the Constitution of 1723.

(31) The "Rawlinson" is the last we mention. This manuscript bears the date 1730, and is in the custody of the Bodlein Library, Oxford. It was published in the "Freemason's Magazine," 1855, and in "Masonic Magazine," 1876. This is said to have been copied from an old manuscript in the possession of Dr. Rawlinson about 1730. The end of the book contains instead of "the contents of this booke," the words are *"the holy contents of this Roll."*

CHAPTER XIV.

The essential features of Freemasonry are universally the same. Its fundamental principles, its distinctive teaching, and its whole scope and spirit are intensely theistical. Comprehended in these principles and teaching are its pre-eminently cosmistic character. This renders it peculiarly cosmopolitan. Hence it is found in every civilized country of the world where liberty of conscience is permitted. In the following pages we give the dates of its introduction into the various countries. We have already treated of its "Revival" in England in the year 1717. From this period it rapidly spread, through not only the British Isles, but extended to the continents of Europe, North and South America, Asia, Africa, and Australasia.

We are furnished with no documentary evidence of the introduction of Freemasonry into the United States; but it appears that it had an existence there as early as the year

(360)

1606. We have historical evidence that charters were received for the whole of Nova Scotia in the year 1621. There was a Grand Lodge of Massachusetts in the year 1740.

Benjamin Franklin was made a Mason in the year 1731, and George Washington was initiated in the year 1752.

Freemasonry appeared in Canada as early as 1760 in the form of Military Lodges, both British and Colonial.

During the Revolutionary War, from the years 1777 to 1778, a chest containing the Lodge Warrant, belonging to the 46th Regiment of Foot (British), was taken by the Americans, but the immortal Washington, with his characteristic chivalry, and as a true brother, had it returned to the Regiment under a flag of truce.

Following are the dates in which Freemasonry was introduced into the different States of the Union:

Connecticut in the year	....	A. D.	1750
Georgia	" "	"	1778
Florida	" "	"	1778
Maryland	" "	"	1765
Massachusetts	" "	"	1733
Michigan	" "	"	1764

New York   in the year ....A. D. 1737
Virginia   "   "   ....   "   1753
Pennsylvania   "   "   ....   "   1734
North Carolina "   "   ....   "   1754
Rhode Island   "   "   ....   "   1757
South Carolina "   "   ....   "   1736
Alabama   "   "   ....   "   1812
New Jersey   "   "   ....   "   1786
New Hampshire   "   "   ....   "   1735
Vermont   "   "   ....   "   1781
Kentucky   "   "   ....   "   1788
Delaware   "   "   ....   "   1765
Ohio   "   "   ....   "   1790
District of Columbia in the year........   "   .1783
Louisiana   in the year ....   "   1793
Tennesse   "   "   ....   "   1796
Indiana   "   "   ....   "   1808
Mississippi   "   "   ....   "   1801
Maine   "   "   ....   "   1762
Missouri   "   " (by the French) "   1797
Texas   "   "   ....   "   1835
Arkansas   "   "   ....   "   1820
Illinois   "   "   ....   "   1805
Wisconsin   "   "   ....   "   1824
Iowa   "   "   ....   "   1841
California   "   "   ....   "   1848
Oregon   "   "   ....   "   1851
Minnesota   "   "   ....   "   1849
Kansas   "   "   ....   "   1855
Nebraska   "   "   ....   "   ˥ ⸯ5
Washington   "   "   ....   "   1858
Colorado   "   "   ....   "   1861
Nevada   "   "   ....   "   1863
West Virginia   "   "   ....   "   1865
Montana   "   "   ....   "   1864
Idaho   "   "   ....   "   1867

Utah	in the year	....	A. D.	1866
Indian Ter.	" "	....	"	1874
Wyoming Ter.	" "	....	"	1868
Dakota Ter.	" "	....	"	1862
New Mexico	" "	....	"	1851
Arizona	" "	....	"	1866

EUROPEAN COUNTRIES.

After the "Revival" in England, Free-masonry was known to exist in the following countries at the dates mentioned:

Sweden and Norway	....	A. D.	1740
Holland	....	"	1731
Belgium	....	"	1833

(It is supposed that the Ancient and Accepted Scottish Rite existed in Belgium as early as 1714.)

Russia	....	A. D.	1732
Poland	....	"	1739
Germany, Saxony	....	"	1729
" Hamburg	....	"	1765
" Frankfort-on-Maine	....	"	1742
Prussia	....	"	1738
Hanover	....	"	1743
Brunswick	....	"	1744
Austria and Hungary	....	"	1731
Switzerland	....	"	1736
Italy, Naples and Sicily	....	"	1750
" Sardinia	....	"	1739
Portugal	....	"	1727
Spain, Gibraltar	....	"	1728
Greece	....	"	1809
Turkey	....	"	1748
Roumania	....	"	1859

ASIA.

India	A. D.	1730
Ceylon	"	1771
Persia	"	1810
China	"	1767
Japan	"	1866

AFRICA.

Egypt	A. D.	1802
Cape Colony	"	1772
West Indies	"	1739
Mexico (Scottish Rite)	"	1810
Central America	"	1763
South America	"	1824

In these pages we have traced the stream of human history from its source downward through the stream of the ages to the present time. We have seen what was the primeval Revelation from God, the Eternal Creator, to man, His creature, whom He formed, in His own image. We have traced the progress of the truth in its various channels of purity and corruption through the different phases and development of human life. We have pointed out the preservation of this truth through the various vicissitudes of human existence. We have traced the glorious facts of Revelation as they had been handed down and preserved in symbol, myth, and

allegory, as they had been preserved in the
"Ancient Mysteries;" and how these great
truths were more and more corrupted as the
centuries rolled on, until at last they sunk
beneath the weight of their own corruption.

We have traced the development and
preservation of the truth in the line of the
Patriarchs from Abraham to David. We
have noted the silent testimony of the Great
Pyramid in Egypt to an important part of
this truth. We have dwelt on the wondrous
structure of the Temple at Jerusalem and
its exalted symbolism, and of the fusion
(to some extent) of Hebrew and Tyrian
thought and cult. We have also treated of
the Roman Colleges of Artificers established
by Numa some seven hundred years before
the Christian era, and how, with certain
modifications, they spread over all the most
civilized countries of Europe and England.
We have also placed before you some of the
distinctive features of the religious Fraternities of the Essenes and Culdees, and the
striking resemblance of many of their usages
to the Masonic Fraternity.

We have also investigated the History and

Organization of the Association of Operative Masons of the Middle Ages, and how that in their outward forms and other features they so closely resembled Freemasonry. We have also treated of the manner in which the Speculative element was introduced into the Operative art, and how, eventually, it became exclusively symbolic or speculative in its character, and how that from this sprung, directly, the present *organization* of Freemasonry.

We now ask is the Fraternity of "Ancient, Free, and Accepted Masons " such a society as would commend itself for acceptance to the best phase of mankind? Before we directly answer this question, let us premise by saying that the Church of the Living God, itself, does not appear in its perfection here, because of the frailty and imperfections, inconsistencies and sinfulness, of its professing members. Neither does Freemasonry present a perfect picture to the world for the same reasons.

The world can judge of Freemasonry by the scope of its principles, and teaching, and by its fruits. Freemasons invite an investigation of these. They have but little to conceal — nothing excepting a few signs, pass-words, and ceremonies — all else is open to the inspection of the world.

We have already said that its fundamental principles are, Belief in one God, the Supreme Architect of the Universe, Redemption, Immortality, and the Resurrection of the body. It is based, likewise, on the broadest principles of toleration, and the recognition of the glorious truth of the universal Brotherhood of Man, founded on the eternal truth of the Fatherhood of God. It is opposed to tyranny in every form in Church and State. It discountenances vice, and exalts and emphasizes virtue. Its universality is apparent in its extending its benefits to men of all nationalities, and religions, and includes in its grand design for good, the family, society, the nation, and the race at large.

It is a system of Symbolism, and its symbols teach the purest and highest truths. It is engaged in erecting a temple — the Temple of Humanity — which it seeks to elevate in its entirety — body, soul, and spirit. In this it recognizes the great truth, that he builds in vain who does not acknowledge and invoke the aid of Him who is the Grand Architect.

In its teachings it employs the facts of nature and of history, with a grandeur and yet a simplicity which is truly striking. Its mission and its duty is to show that the essence of love is self-sacrifice, and to this end it inculcates tenderness in ministrations, inspires ennobling aspirations, intensifies loyalty in friendship, and stimulates truth and honor in all the relations of life. It invokes and deepens the sentiment of good-will to all mankind.

That all this is practical is evidenced by the existence of the splendid active charities it maintains for the aged, the widow, and the orphan; and is further evidenced by the sympathy, care, and help given to the poor and the needy. All this, and much more, deservedly win utterances of commendation even from those who are not of the Craft. Universal benevolence are the tenets of Freemasonry, in contrast to the frigid, sordid selfishness which debases the nobler

traits of man's character. It places prominently in its beautiful ritual, impressive
ceremonies and far-reaching philosophy, the
unfathomable, exhaustless love of God.

As the Fraternity of Freemasons is in-
comparably the most ancient of all the
Fraternities now in the world, so there is
now none existing which teaches such sublime morality. In this it is truly the handmaid of religion. Intemperance, immorality,
disloyalty to citizenship, irreverence towards
sacred things, impiety, and profanity are
wholly opposed to the spirit and teaching of
Freemasonry. And that contemptible, cow-
ardly, and unmanly habit of backbiting and
villifying the character of the absent, is, in
the strongest manner, condemned by the
express teaching of the Fraternity. Slander
in every shape is condemned as devilish, and
is most repugnant to the whole spirit of
Freemasonry.

Instead of this, it inculcates that beautiful
spirit of charity which, while it does not
condone nor palliate vice, yet "covers the
multitude of sins."

The Golden Rule of the Saviour, "Do

unto others as you would wish they should
do unto you," is made prominent in the whole
teaching of the Craft; and the maxims of
mutual duty and obligation which man owes
to his fellowmen is emphatically inculcated.

Is it any wonder then, in view of these
facts, that the Institution should reckon
among her hosts, the pious, the religious, the
philanthropist, the patriot, the warrior, the
jurist, the philosopher, the divine, the me-
chanic, the artist, men of all grades and
ranks of life who prize virtue, stimulate
progress and civilization, and cherish true
liberty.

On this plane Freemasonry moves majes-
tically along with the stream of the ages,
molding the character of men, recognizing
her indebtedness to the past, her obligation
to the present and the future, realizing her
grand scope and broad field of mission,
keeping true to her ancient landmarks,
scattering benediction in her path in active
benevolence and charity to all who come
within the sphere of her influence.   And as
each member of the Craft, mindful of his
individual responsibility, acts faithfully his

part in the Lodge on earth, awaits the
Supreme Master's mandate summoning him
to the Lodge in heaven, looks forward with
bright anticipations, and holy aspirations, to
that event which shall admit him to the
glorious Brotherhood of the Redeemed in
the presence of the Great. "I AM" where
love, joy, and immortality shall be his portion for ever.

SO MOTE IT BE.

THE END.

INDEX.

A

(373)

B

C

T

www.ingramcontent.com/pod-product-compliance
Lightning Source LLC
Chambersburg PA
CBHW021613270326
41931CB00008B/675